Rachel Walter Hinkle Shoemaker

Young folks' recitations

Rachel Walter Hinkle Shoemaker

Young folks' recitations

ISBN/EAN: 9783337768560

Printed in Europe, USA, Canada, Australia, Japan

Cover: Foto ©ninafisch / pixelio.de

More available books at **www.hansebooks.com**

Young Folks' Recitations

NUMBER 1

Designed for Young People of Five Years

COMPILED BY
Mrs. J. W. Shoemaker

PUBLICATION DEPARTMENT
The National School of Elocution and Oratory
PHILADELPHIA
1888

Entered according to Act of Congress, in the year 1884, by
THE NATIONAL SCHOOL OF ELOCUTION AND ORATORY,

Philadelphia.

PREFACE.

THIS little volume is designed for children between the ages of five and fifteen years.

The need, as well as the numerous inquiries for a work of this kind, has led to the preparation of the present compilation.

Our resources for collecting that which is fresh, varied, and vigorous are many; and, while engaged in the task of arranging, three things were kept prominently in view: first, that the selections should neither be long nor tedious; second, that there should be an abundant variety; and, third, that the tone or character should be healthful. Hence, there are short pieces both of poetry and prose, some treating of plant and animal life, some of childhood pleasures, some brimming with innocent fun, some filled with patriotic fervor, some with bits of philosophy, and others designed to inspire the soul with motives toward truth, honor, right, and duty.

A few dialogues and acting tableaux are appended, and thus through its adaptability it is believed that the book will meet the wants of children for the merry-makings in the home circle, for church anniversaries, and for school exhibitions. Such then is the style and character of this collection of Readings and Recitations which we offer to you, the Young Folks of our Beloved Land, trusting you may find in it much to gratify and please, and, above all, that which will lead your minds and hearts to thoughts Beautiful, Pure, and Good.

Mrs. J. W. Shoemaker.

Philadelphia, January 1st, 1884.

CONTENTS.

Success in Life	*James A. Garfield*	7
Do Something		9
How Cyrus Laid the Cable		10
Little by Little		11
What the Winds Bring	*Edmund Clarence Stedman*	12
The Two Roads		12
The Boy's Complaint		13
Never Say Fail		14
Farewell of the Birds	*H. K. P.*	15
Boys Wanted		17
Do Right		17
Good Deeds	*Dr. T. Chalmers*	18
The Two Commands		18
A Christmas Eve Adventure	*M. M.*	19
The Way to Do It	*Mary Mapes Dodge*	21
Speak the Truth		22
Battle Bunny—Malvern Hill	*Bret Harte*	23
A Child's Wisdom		25
The Nobility of Labor	*Rev. Orville Dewey*	26
Lazy Daisy		27
The Moon and the Child	*George Jacque*	28
The Sparkling Bowl	*John Pierpont*	29
Sweet Peas	*Lilian Payson*	30
The King and the Child	*Eugene J. Hall*	31
Do You Know How Many Stars?		33
The Fathers of the Republic	*Everett*	34
A Horse's Petition to His Driver		34
Antony on the Death of Cæsar	*Shakespeare*	35
Sour Grapes		35
Be in Earnest	*Bulwer*	36
Suppose	*Phœbe Cary*	37
The Squirrel's Lesson		38
Homesick		39
War Inevitable	*Patrick Henry*	41
That Calf	*Phœbe Cary*	42
Johnny the Stout		44
What the Minutes Say		45
The Little Boy's Lament		46
Nature	*Hugh Miller*	47
The Boy and the Frog		47
Homœopathic Soup		49

CONTENTS.

Lines to Kate		50
Grand Scheme of Emigration		52
Brave and True	Henry Downton	53
The Cobbler		54
What's the Matter?	H. K. P.	55
Peaceable Secession	Webster	56
Baby's Soliloquy		57
A Tribute to Water	John B. Gough	58
Grandpapa's Spectacles		59
Sin	Baxter	60
February Twenty-second	Joy Allison	61
The Stolen Custard		62
Somebody's Mother	Macmillan	63
Willie's Breeches	Etta G. Salsbury	64
Work	Thomas Carlyle	65
Loveliness	Maria Lacey	66
Being a Boy	Charles Dudley Warner	67
We Must All Scratch		69
Blowing Bubbles	Rev. O. F. Starkey	70
When the Frost is on the Punkin		72
America's Obligations to England	Colonel Barre	73
Planting Himself to Grow		74
Dignity in Labor	Newman Hall	75
Where Did You Come From, Baby?	George Macdonald	76
A Little Boy's Troubles	Carlotta Perry	77
Notes from a Battle-field	S. C. Stone	79
Three Good Doctors	S. W. Duffield, D. D.	81
On Conquering America	Lord Chatham	82
The Indian Brave	Francis S. Smith	83
Johnny's Pocket		84
Six o'clock P. M.		85
A Sollum Fac'		86
The Little Light		87
The Bird and the Baby	Alfred Tennyson	88
The Return from Battle		89
The American Flag	A. P. Putnam	90
Lost Tommy	Mrs. Julia M. Dana	91
The Foolish Harebell	George Macdonald	93
Only a Baby Small	Matthias Barr	94
Brutus on the Death of Cæsar	Shakespeare	95

MISCELLANEOUS.

Three Little Mushrooms	96
Real Elocution	97
Knowing the Circumstances	101
A Song of the States	103

SUCCESS IN LIFE.

POETS may be born, but success is made; therefore let me beg of you, in the outset of your career, to dismiss from your minds all ideas of succeeding by luck.

There is no more common thought among young people than that foolish one that by and by something will turn up by which they will suddenly achieve fame or fortune. Luck is an ignis fatuus. You may follow it to ruin, but not to success. The great Napoleon, who believed in his destiny, followed it until he saw his star go down in blackest night, when the Old Guard perished around him, and Waterloo was lost. A pound of pluck is worth a ton of luck.

Young men talk of trusting to the spur of the occasion. That trust is vain. Occasion cannot make spurs. If you expect to wear spurs, you must win them. If you wish to use them, you must buckle them to your own heels before you go into the fight. Any success you may achieve is not worth the having unless you fight for it. Whatever you win in life you must conquer by your own efforts, and then it is yours—a part of yourself.

Again: in order to have any success in life, or any worthy success, you must resolve to carry into your work a fullness of knowledge—not merely a sufficiency, but more than a sufficiency. Be fit for more than the thing you are now doing. Let every one know that you have a reserve in yourself; that you have more power than you are now using. If you are not too large for the place you occupy, you are too small for it. How full our country is of bright examples, not only of those who occupy some proud eminence in public life, but in every place you may find men going on with steady nerve, attracting the attention of their fellow-citizens, and carving out for themselves names and fortunes from small and humble beginnings and in the face of formidable obstacles.

Let not poverty stand as an obstacle in your way. Poverty is uncomfortable, as I can testify; but nine times out of ten the best thing that can happen to a young man is to be tossed overboard, and compelled to sink or swim for himself. In all my acquaintance, I have never known one to be drowned who was worth the saving. This would not be wholly true in any country but one of political equality like ours.

The reason is this: In the aristocracies of the Old World, wealth and society are built up like the strata of rock which compose the crust of the earth. If a boy be born in the lowest stratum of life, it is almost impossible for him to rise through this hard crust into the higher ranks; but in this country it is not so. The strata of our society resemble rather the ocean, where every drop, even the lowest, is free to mingle with all others, and may shine at last on the crest of the highest wave. This is the glory of our country, and you need not fear that there are any obstacles which will prove too great for any brave heart.

In giving you being, God locked up in your nature certain forces and capabilities. What will you do with them? Look at the mechanism of a clock. Take off the pendulum and ratchet, and the wheels go rattling down and all its force is expended in a moment; but properly balanced and regulated, it will go on, letting out its force tick by tick, measuring hours and days, and doing faithfully the service for which it was designed. I implore you to cherish and guard and use well the forces that God has given to you. You may let them run down in a year, if you will. Take off the strong curb of discipline and morality, and you will be an old man before your twenties are passed. Preserve these forces. Do not burn them out with brandy, or waste them in idleness and crime. Do not destroy them. Do not use them unworthily. Save and protect them, that they may save for you fortune and fame. Honestly resolve to do this, and you will be an honor to yourself and to your country.

JAMES A. GARFIELD.

DO SOMETHING.

IF the world seems cold to you,
   Kindle fires to warm it!
Let their comfort hide from you
   Winters that deform it.

Hearts as frozen as your own
   To that radiance gather;
You will soon forget to moan,
   "Ah! the cheerless weather."

If the world's a vale of tears,
   Smile till rainbows span it;
Breathe the love that life endears—
   Clear from clouds to fan it.

Of our gladness lend a gleam
   Unto souls that shiver;
Show them how dark sorrow's stream
   Blends with hope's bright river!

HOW CYRUS LAID THE CABLE.

COME, listen to my song, it is no silly fable,
    'Tis all about the mighty cord they call the Atlantic Cable.

Bold Cyrus Field, said he, "I have a pretty notion
That I could run a telegraph across the Atlantic Ocean."

And all the people laughed and said they'd like to see him do it;
He might get "half seas over," but never would go through it.

To carry out his foolish plan he never would be able;
He might as well go hang himself with his Atlantic Cable.

But Cyrus was a valiant man, a fellow of decision,
And heeded not their careless words, their laughter and derision.

Twice did his bravest efforts fail, yet his mind was stable;
He wasn't the man to break his heart because he broke his cable.

"Once more, my gallant boys," said he; "three times," —you know the fable.
"I'll make it thirty," muttered he, "but what I'll lay the cable."

Hurrah! hurrah! again hurrah! what means this great commotion?
Hurrah! hurrah! The cable's laid across the Atlantic Ocean.

Loud ring the bells, for flashing through ten thousand
    leagues of water,
Old Mother England's benison salutes her eldest daugh-
    ter.

O'er all the land the tidings spread, and soon in every
    nation,
They'll hear about the cable with profoundest admira-
    tion.

Long live the gallant souls who helped our noble Cyrus;
And may their courage, faith, and zeal, with emulation
    fire us.

And may we honor, evermore, the manly, bold and stable,
And tell our sons, to make them brave, how Cyrus laid
    the Cable.

LITTLE BY LITTLE.

ONE step and then another, and the longest walk is
    ended;
One stitch and then another, and the widest rent is
    mended;
One brick upon another, and the highest wall is made;
One flake upon another, and the deepest snow is laid.

Then do not frown nor murmur at the work you have to
    do,
Or say that such a mighty task you never can get through;
But just endeavor, day by day, another point to gain,
And soon the mountain that you feared will prove to be
    a plain.

WHAT THE WINDS BRING.

WHICH is the wind that brings the cold?
    The north-wind, Freddy, and all the snow,
And the sheep will scamper into the fold,
    When the north begins to blow.

Which is the wind that brings the heat?
    The south-wind, Katy; and corn will grow,
And peaches redden for you to eat,
    When the south begins to blow.

Which is the wind that brings the rain?
    The east-wind, Arty; and farmers know
That cows come shivering up the lane
    When the east begins to blow.

Which is the wind that brings the flowers?
    The west-wind, Bessy; and soft and low,
The birdies sing in the summer hours
    When the west begins to blow.
              EDMUND CLARENCE STEDMAN.

THE TWO ROADS.

WHERE two ways meet the children stand,
    A fair, broad road on either hand;
One leads to Right, and one to Wrong;
    So runs the song.

Which will you choose, each lass and lad?
The right or left, the good or bad?
One leads to Right, and one to Wrong;
    So runs the song.

THE BOY'S COMPLAINT.

"OH! never mind, they're only boys;"
   'Tis thus the people say,
And they hustle us and jostle us,
   And drive us out the way.

They never give us half our rights:
   I know that this is so;
Ain't I a boy? and can't I see
   The way that these things go?

The little girls are petted all,
   Called "honey," "dear," and "sweet,"
But boys are cuffed at home and school,
   And knocked about the street.

My sister has her rags and dolls
   Strewn all about the floor,
While old dog Growler dares not put
   His nose inside the door.

And if I go upon the porch
   In hopes to have a play,
Some one calls out, "Hollo, young chap,
   Take that noisy dog away!"

My hoop is used to build a fire,
   My ball is thrown aside;
And mother let the baby have
   My top, because it cried.

If company should come at night,
   The boys can't sit up late;
And if they come to dinner, then
   The boys, of course, must wait.

If anything is raw or burned·
  It falls to us, no doubt;
And if the cake or pudding's short,
  We have to go without.

If there are fireworks, we can't get
  A place to see at all;
And when the soldiers come along
  We're crowded to the wall.

Whoever wants an errand done,
  We always have to scud;
Whoever wants the sidewalk, we
  Are crowded in the mud.

'Tis hurry-scurry, here and there,
  Without a moment's rest,
And we scarcely get a "Thank you," if
  We do our very best.

But never mind, boys—we will be
  The grown men by and by;
Then I suppose 'twill be our turn
  To snub the smaller boy.

NEVER SAY FAIL.

IN life's rosy morning,
  In manhood's pride,
Let this be your motto,
  Your footsteps to guide:
In storms and in sunshine,
  Whatever assail,
We'll onward and conquer,
  And never say fail.

FAREWELL OF THE BIRDS.

TO Jennie at play in the garden,
   To Bessie and Maud on the hill,
To all the sweet children that frolic
   So gayly by brooklet and rill
     We are coming to-day.
     But, hush! Never tell!
     We are coming, I say,
       To bid you farewell!

You welcomed us early in spring,
   With laughter and shoutings so sweet;
To your childhood our music we bring,
   You scatter your crumbs at our feet.
     You love us, we know.
     Now listen, 'tis true:
     We're sorry to sing
       This farewell to you.

We've led you full many a race
   O'er hillside and valley and dell;
We've beckoned you on to the forest,
   And shown you where wild flowers dwell;
     We've twittered and sung
       New songs every day;
     We'll give a grand chorus
       E'er flying away.

Where berries are ripest and sweetest,
   Where grapes their rich perfume distill,
We enticed you by flutter and music,
   Your little school-baskets to fill.

We showed you our nest,
In shadiest nook;
We trusted your honor
To take but a look.

But the berries are gone from the roadside,
The flowers hold the dew-drops no more;
The grapes from the vine have been gathered,
And, children, our play-time is o'er.
Good-bye, then, to Bessie,
To Clara, and May,
To all who are kind
To the birds at their play.

We go where the days are all sunny,
The breezes all softened and bland,
Where flowers and fruits never fail,
In a far-away, dreamy Southland.
But we love you all as well.
Now list while we sing:
We are sure to fly back
At the coming of spring.

Yes, in the spring time again
We'll build near your homes in the tree;
We hope that each laughing-eyed urchin
And maiden will be there to see.
But now we must go;
Oh! pray, do not cry,
As upward and onward
We warble, Good-bye.

H. K. P.

BOYS WANTED.

Boys of spirit, boys of will,
    Boys of muscle, brain, and power,
Fit to cope with anything,
    These are wanted every hour.

Not the weak and whining drones,
    Who all troubles magnify;
Not the watchword of "I can't,"
    But the nobler one, "I'll try."

Do whate'er you have to do
    With a true and earnest zeal;
Bend your sinews to the task,
    "Put your shoulder to the wheel."

Though your duty may be hard,
    Look not on it as an ill;
If it be an honest task,
    Do it with an honest will.

In the workshop, on the farm,
    At the desk, where'er you be,
From your future efforts, boys,
    Comes a nation's destiny.

DO RIGHT.

Do what conscience says is right;
    Do what reason says is best;
Do with all your mind and might;
    Do your duty and be blest.

GOOD DEEDS.

THOUSANDS of men breathe, move, and live, pass off the stage of life, and are heard of no more. Why? They do not partake of good in this world, and none were blessed by them; none could point to them as the means of their redemption; not a line they wrote, not a word they spake, could be recalled; and so they perished; their light went out in darkness, and they were not remembered more than insects of yesterday. Will you thus live and die, O man immortal? Live for something. Do good, and leave behind you a monument of virtue that the storm of time can never destroy. Write your name, in kindness, in love, and mercy, on the hearts of thousands you come in contact with year by year: you will never be forgotten. No! Your name, your deeds, will be as legible on the hearts you leave behind you as the stars on the brow of evening. Good deeds will shine as the stars of heaven.

Dr. T. Chalmers.

THE TWO COMMANDS.

THIS is the first and great command:
    To love thy God above;
And this the second: As thyself
    Thy neighbor thou shalt love.
Who is thy neighbor? He who wants
    A help which thou canst give;
And both the law and prophets say,
    This do and thou shalt live.

A CHRISTMAS EVE ADVENTURE.

ONCE on a time, in a queer little town
   On the shore of the Zuyder Zee,
When all the good people were fast asleep,
   A strange thing happened to me!

Alone, the night before Christmas,
   I sat by the glowing fire,
Watching the flame as it rose and fell,
   While the sparks shot high and higher.

Suddenly one of these sparks began
   To flicker and glimmer and wink
Like a big bright eye, till I hardly knew
   What to do or to say or to think.

Quick as a flash, it changed to a face,
   And what in the world did I see
But dear old Santa Claus nodding his head,
   And waving his hand to me!

"Oh! follow me, follow me!" soft he cried,—
   And up through the chimney with him
I mounted, not daring to utter a word
   Till we stood on the chimney's rim.

"Now tell me, I beg you, dear Santa Claus,
   Where am I going with you?"
He laughingly answered, "Why, don't you know?
   To travel the wide world through!

"From my crystal palace, far in the North,
   I have come since dark,—and see
These curious things for the little folk
   Who live on the Zuyder Zee."

Then seating himself in his reindeer sledge,
   And drawing me down by his side,
He whistled, and off on the wings of the wind
   We flew for our midnight ride.

But first, such comical presents he left
   For the little Dutch girls and boys,—
Onions and sausages, wooden-faced dolls,
   Cheeses and gingerbread toys!

Away we hurried far to the South,
   To the beautiful land of France;
And there we showered the loveliest gifts,—
   Flaxen-haired dolls that could dance,

Soldiers that marched at the word of command,
   Necklaces, bracelets, and rings,
Tiny gold watches, all studded with gems,
   And hundreds of exquisite things.

Crossing the Channel, we made a short call
   In Scotland and Ireland, too;
Left a warm greeting for England and Wales,
   Then over the ocean we flew

Straight to America, where by myself,
   Perched on a chimney high,
I watched him scramble and bustle about
   Between the earth and the sky.

Many a stocking he filled to the brim,
   And numberless Christmas trees
Burst into bloom at his magical touch!
   Then all of a sudden, a breeze

Caught us and bore us away to the South,
  And afterward blew us "out West;"
And never till dawn peeped over the hills
  Did we stop for a moment's rest.

"Christmas is coming!" he whispered to me,
  You can see his smile in the sky,—
I wish Merry Christmas to all the world!
  My work is over,—good-bye!"

Like a flash he was gone, and I was alone,—
  For all of this happened to me
Once on a time, in a queer little town
  On the shore of the Zuyder Zee!   M. M.

THE WAY TO DO IT.

I'LL tell you how I speak a piece:
  First, I make my bow;
Then I bring my words out clear
  And plain as I know how.

Next, I throw my hands up—so!
  Then I lift my eyes:
That's to let my hearers know
  Something doth surprise.

Next, I grin and show my teeth,
  Nearly every one,
Shake my shoulders, hold my sides:
  That's the sign of fun.

Next, I start, and knit my brows,
  Hold my head erect:
Something's wrong, you see, and I
  Decidedly object.

Then I wabble at my knees,
  Clutch at shadows near,
Tremble well from top to toe:
  That's the sign of fear.

Now I start, and with a leap,
  Seize an airy dagger.
"Wretch!" I cry: That's tragedy,
  Every soul to stagger.

Then I let my voice grow faint,
  Gasp, and hold my breath,
Tumble down and plunge about:
  That's a villain's death.

Quickly then I come to life,
  Perfectly restored;
With a bow my speech is done.
  Now you'll please applaud.
                MARY MAPES DODGE.

SPEAK THE TRUTH.

SPEAK the truth!
  Speak it boldly, never fear,
Speak it so that all may hear,
In the end it shall appear
Truth is best in age and youth;
  Speak the truth.

BATTLE BUNNY—MALVERN HILL.

[After the men were ordered to lie down, a white rabbit, which had been hopping hither and thither over the field swept by grape and musketry, took refuge among the skirmishers, in the breast of a corporal.]

BUNNY, lying in the grass,
   Saw the shiny column pass,
Saw the starry banner fly,
Saw the chargers fret and fume,
Saw the flapping hat and plume—
Saw them with his moist and shy,
Most unspeculative eye.
Thinking only, in the dew,
That it was a fine review—
Till a flash, not all of steel,
Where the rolling caisson's wheel
Brought a rumble and a roar
Rolling down that velvet floor,
And like blows of autumn flail
Sharply threshed the iron hail.

Bunny, thrilled by unknown fears,
Raised his soft and pointed ears,
Mumbled his prehensile lip,
Quivered his pulsating hip,
As the sharp, vindictive yell
Rose above the screaming shell:
Thought the world and all its men,
All the charging squadrons meant
All were rabbit hunters then,
All to capture him intent.
Bunny was not much to blame;
Wiser folk have thought the same—
Wiser folk, who think they spy
Every ill begins with " I."

Wildly ranting here and there,
Bunny sought the freer air,
Till he hopped below the hill,
And saw lying, close and still,
Men with muskets in their hands.
Never Bunny understands
That hypocrisy of sleep,
In the vigils grim they keep,
As recumbent on that spot
They elude the level shot.

One—a grave and quiet man,
Thinking of his wife and child
Where the Androscoggin smiled—
Felt the little rabbit creep,
Nestling by his arm and side.
Wakened from strategic sleep,
To that soft appeal replied,
Drew him to his blackened breast,
And—
 But you have guessed the rest.
Softly o'er that chosen pair
Omnipresent Love and Care

Drew a mightier Hand and Arm,
Shielding them from every harm;
Right and left the bullets waved,
Saves the savior for the saved.

Who believes that equal grace
God extends in every place,
Little difference he scans
'Twixt a rabbit's God and man's.

Bret Harte.

A CHILD'S WISDOM.

'TWAS the hour of prayer, and the farmer stood,
   With a thankful heart and a lowly mind,
And prayed to the Author of every good,
   That the Father of all would be very kind
And bless His creatures with raiment and food.
That His blessing each day might be renewed,
That every want might find relief,
And plenty for hunger, joy for grief,
Be measured out by the merciful One,
To all who suffered beneath the sun.

The prayer concluded, the godly man
   Went forth in peace to inspect his farm ;
And by his side, delighted ran,
   Blooming with every healthful charm,
A little son, a sprightly boy,
Whose home was love and whose life was joy.
And they rambled over the golden fields,
And the father said "The harvest yields
A plentiful crop, my son, this year,
My barns are too small for the grain, I fear."

And they wandered on through row upon row,
   Of plumy sheaves, till at length the child,
With earnest look and a brighter glow
   On his shining face, looked up and smiled,
And said, " My father, do you not pray
For the poor and needy every day,
That the good God would give the hungry food?"
" I do, my son." " Well, I think as you plead,"
His eye waxed bright, for his soul shone through it,
" That God, if He had your wheat, would do it."

THE NOBILITY OF LABOR.

I CALL upon those whom I address to stand up for the nobility of labor. It is Heaven's great ordinance for human improvement. Let not that great ordinance be broken down. What do I say? It is broken down; and it has been broken down for ages. Let it, then, be built up again; here, if anywhere, on these shores of a new world—of a new civilization. But how, I may be asked, is it broken down? Do not men toil? it may be said. They do, indeed, toil; but they, too, generally do it because they must. Many submit to it as, in some sort, a degrading necessity; and they desire nothing so much on earth as escape from it. They fulfill the great law of labor in the letter, but break it in the spirit; fulfill it with the muscle, but break it with the mind. To some field of labor, mental or manual, every idler should fasten, as a chosen and coveted theatre of improvement. But so is he not impelled to do, under the teachings of our imperfect civilization. On the contrary, he sits down, folds his hands, and blesses himself in his idleness. This way of thinking is the heritage of the absurd and unjust feudal system, under which serfs labored, and gentlemen spent their lives in fighting and feasting. It is time that this opprobrium of toil were done away. Ashamed to toil, art thou? Ashamed of thy dingy workshop and dusty labor-field; of thy hard hands, scarred with service more honorable than that of war; of thy soiled and weather-stained garments, on which Mother Nature has embroidered, 'midst sun and rain, 'midst fire and steam, her own heraldic honors? Ashamed of these tokens and titles, and envious of the flaunting robes of imbecile idleness and vanity? It is treason to Nature—it is impiety to Heaven—it is breaking Heaven's great ordinance. TOIL, I repeat—TOIL, either of the brain, or of the heart, or of the hand, is the only true manhood, the only true nobility!

REV. ORVILLE DEWEY.

LAZY DAISY.

LITTLE Daisy is so lazy
    This is what she does;
Just as soon as breakfast's eaten
    Off to bed she goes.

Lazy Daisy ne'er was seen
    Reading in a book,
But she loves to lie and sleep
    In a sunny nook.

"Daisy, come and play with me,"
    Little Ethel cries;
Daisy sleeps and nods away,
    Does n't wink her eyes.

Daisy, though she's three years old,
    Cannot tell her name;
Does n't know her A, B, C:
    Isn't it a shame?

But she sings one little song,
    Very soft and pretty:
Purr-purr-purr the whole day long—
    Daisy is a kitty.

THE MOON AND THE CHILD.

A LITTLE child one winter night,
    Ere she was put to bed,
Went out and saw the full clear moon,
    And in she ran and said—

"Mamma! mamma! come here! come quick!
    Mamma! God's gone to bed,
And has not put His candle out!
    "Hush, child!" the mother said,

"God does not go to bed like us,
    Nor does He need to sleep."
"And does He sit up all the night,
    Watch over us to keep?"

"He watches o'er us night and day,
    But needs no light to see."
"No light, mamma?" "No light, my child."
    "Mamma, how can it be?"

"He makes the owls to see by night,
    As if the daylight shone;
And darkness is to Him as light,
    And eyes He needeth none."

"No eyes!—then is He blind, mamma?"
    "No, child, He sees so well,
That everything is seen by Him
    In heaven, earth, and hell."

"How strange, mamma, that He should see
    When He's so far away."
"Not far, for He is everywhere,
    And with us night and day."

"Why don't we see Him then, mamma?"
"I cannot tell you how,
But this I know, you cannot see
　The air you're breathing now;

"And neither can you see my soul,
　Nor yet your own, I ween.
It is not then so very strange
　That God should not be seen.

"Now go to bed, and ere you go
　To God your prayers say,
That He may please to spare your life
　To see another day."
　　　　　　　　　GEORGE JACQUE.

THE SPARKLING BOWL.

THOU sparkling bowl! thou sparkling bowl!
　Though lips of bards thy brim may press,
And eyes of beauty o'er thee roll,
　And song and dance thy power confess,
I will not touch thee; for there clings
A scorpion to thy side that stings!

Thou crystal glass! like Eden's tree,
　Thy melted ruby tempts the eye,
And, as from that, there comes from thee
　The voice, "Thou shalt not surely die."
I dare not lift thy liquid gem;
A snake is twisted round thy stem!

What though of gold the goblet be,
  Emboss'd with branches of the vine,
Beneath whose burnish'd leaves we see
  Such clusters as pour'd out the wine?
Among those leaves an adder hangs!
I fear him;—for I've felt his fangs.

Ye gracious clouds! ye deep, cold wells!
  Ye gems, from mossy rocks that drip!
Springs, that from earth's mysterious cells
  Gush o'er your granite basin's lip!
To you I look;—your largess give,
And I will drink of you, and live.

JOHN PIERPONT.

SWEET PEAS.

"PLEASE wear my rosebud, for love, papa,"
  Said Phebe with eyes so blue.
"This sprig of myrtle put with it, papa,
  To tell of my love," said Prue.
Said Patience, "This heart's-ease shall whisper, papa,
  Forget not my love is true."

Papa looked into the laughing eyes,
And answered, to each little girl's surprise:
"My darlings, I thank you, but dearer than these—
Forgive me—far dearer are bonnie sweet peas!"
Then he clasped them to his heart so true,
And whispered, "Sweet P's—Phebe, Patience, and Prue!"

LILIAN PAYSON.

THE KING AND THE CHILD.

THE sunlight shone on walls of stone
    And towers sublime and tall;
King Alfred sat upon his throne
    Within his council hall.

And glancing o'er the splendid throng,
    With grave and solemn face,
To where his noble vassals stood,
    He saw a vacant place.

"Where is the Earl of Holderness?"
    With anxious look, he said.
"Alas, O King!" a courtier cried,
    "The noble Earl is dead!"

Before the monarch could express
    The sorrow that he felt,
A soldier with a war-worn face
    Approached the throne and knelt.

"My sword," he said, "has ever been,
    O King! at thy command,
And many a proud and haughty Dane
    Has fallen by my hand.

"I've fought beside thee in the field,
    And 'neath the greenwood tree;
It is but fair for thee to give
    Yon vacant place to me."

"It is not just," a statesman cried,
    "This soldier's prayer to hear,
My wisdom has done more for thee
    Than either sword or spear.

"The victories of the council hall
    Have made thee more renown
Than all the triumphs of the field
    Have given to thy crown.

"My name is known in every land,
    My talents have been thine,
Bestow this Earldom, then, on me,
    For it is justly mine."

Yet, while before the monarch's throne
    These men contending stood,
A woman crossed the floor who wore
    The weeds of widowhood.

And slowly to King Alfred's feet
    A fair-haired boy she led—
"O King! this is the rightful heir
    Of Holderness," she said.

"Helpless he comes to claim his own,
    Let no man do him wrong,
For he is weak and fatherless,
    And thou art just and strong."

"What strength of power," the statesman cried,
    "Could such a judgment bring?
Can such a feeble child as this
    Do aught for thee, O King?

"When thou hast need of brawny arms
    To draw thy deadly bows,
When thou art wanting crafty men
    To crush thy mortal foes."

With earnest voice the fair young boy
   Replied: "I cannot fight,
But I can pray to God, O King!
   And Heaven can give thee might!"

The King bent down and kissed the child,
   The courtiers turned away.
"The heritage is thine," he said,
   "Let none their right gainsay.

"Our swords may cleave the casques of men,
   Our blood may stain the sod,
But what are human strength and power
   Without the help of God!"

EUGENE J. HALL.

DO YOU KNOW HOW MANY STARS?

DO you know how many stars
   There are shining in the sky?
Do you know how many clouds
   Every day go floating by?
God in Heaven has counted all,
He would miss one should it fall.

Do you know how many children
   Go to little beds at night,
And without a care or sorrow,
   Wake up in the morning light?
God in Heaven each name can tell,
Knows you, too, and knows you well.

THE FATHERS OF THE REPUBLIC.

TO be cold and breathless, to feel not and speak not—this is not the end of existence to the men who have breathed their spirits into the institutions of their country, who have stamped their characters on the pillars of the age, who have poured their hearts' blood into the channels of the public prosperity.

Tell me, ye who tread the sods of yon sacred height, is Warren dead? Can you not still see him—not pale and prostrate, the blood of his gallant heart pouring out of his ghastly wound, but moving resplendent over the field of honor, with the rose of heaven upon his cheek and the fire of liberty in his eye?

Tell me, ye who make your pious pilgrimage to the shades of Vernon, is Washington indeed shut up in that cold and narrow house? That which made these men, and men like these, cannot die.

The hand that traced the charter of independence is, indeed, motionless; the eloquent lips that sustained it are hushed; but the lofty spirits that conceived, resolved and maintained it, and which alone, to such men, make it life to live—these cannot expire.

EVERETT.

A HORSE'S PETITION TO HIS DRIVER.

UP the hill, whip me not; down the hill, hurry me not; in the stable, forget me not; of hay and corn, rob me not; of clean water, stint me not; with sponge and brush, neglect me not; of soft, dry bed, deprive me not; if sick or cold, chill me not; with bit and reins, oh! jerk me not; and when you are angry, strike me not.

ANTONY ON THE DEATH OF CÆSAR.

GOOD friends, sweet friends, let me not stir you up
To such a sudden flood of mutiny.
They, that have done this deed, are honorable:
What private griefs they have, alas! I know not,
That made them do 't; they are wise and honorable,
And will, no doubt, with reasons answer you.
I came not, friends, to steal away your hearts;
I am no orator, as Brutus is;
But as you know me all, a plain, blunt man,
That love my friend, and that they know full well
That gave me public leave to speak of him.
For I have neither wit, nor words, nor worth,
Action, nor utterance, nor the power of speech,
To stir men's blood: I only speak right on;
I tell you that which you yourselves do know;
Show you sweet Cæsar's wounds, poor, poor dumb mouths,
And bid them speak for me: But were I Brutus
And Brutus Antony, there were an Antony
Would ruffle up your spirits, and put a tongue
In every wound of Cæsar, that should move
The stones of Rome to rise and mutiny.
SHAKESPEARE.

SOUR GRAPES.

A FOX was trotting on one day,
    And just above his head
He spied a vine of luscious grapes,
    Rich, ripe, and purple-red;
Eager he tried to snatch the fruit,
    But, ah! it was too high!

Poor Reynard had to give it up,
  And, heaving a deep sigh,
He curl'd his nose and said, " Dear me !
  I would not waste an hour
Upon such mean and common fruit—
  I'm sure those grapes are sour !"
'Tis thus we often wish thro' life,
  When seeking wealth and pow'r ;
And when we fail, say, like the fox,
  We're " sure the grapes are sour !"

BE IN EARNEST.

NEVER be ashamed to say, " I do not know." Men will then believe you when you say, " I do know."

Never be ashamed to say, " I can't afford it ;" " I can't afford to waste time in the idleness to which you invite me," or " I can't afford the money you ask me to spend." Never affect to be other than you are—either wiser or richer.

Learn to say " No " with decision ; " Yes " with caution. " No " with decision whenever it resists temptation ; " Yes " with caution whenever it implies a promise ; for a promise once given is a bond inviolable.

A man is already of consequence in the world when it is known that we can implicitly rely upon him. Often have I known a man to be preferred in stations of honor and profit because he had this reputation : when he said he knew a thing, he knew it ; and when he said he would do a thing, he did it.

BULWER.

SUPPOSE.

SUPPOSE, my little lady,
    Your doll should break her head,
Could you make it whole by crying
    Till eyes and nose are red?
And wouldn't it be pleasanter
    To treat it as a joke,
And say you're glad 'twas dolly's
    And not your head that broke?

Suppose you're dressed for walking
    And the rain comes pouring down,
Will it clear off any sooner
    Because you scold and frown?
And wouldn't it be nicer
    For you to smile than pout,
And so make sunshine in the house
    When there is none without?

Suppose your task, my little man,
    Is very hard to get,
Will it make it any easier
    For you to sit and fret?
And wouldn't it be nicer
    Than waiting like a dunce,
To go to work in earnest
    And learn the thing at once?

And suppose the world don't please you,
    Nor the way some people do,
Do you think the whole creation
    Will be altered just for you?

And isn't it, my boy or girl,
  The bravest, wisest plan
Whatever comes or doesn't come,
  To do the best you can?

PHŒBE CARY.

THE SQUIRREL'S LESSON.

TWO little squirrels, out in the sun,
  One gathered nuts, and the other had none;
"Time enough yet," his constant refrain;
"Summer is still only just on the wane."

Listen, my child, while I tell you his fate:
He roused him at last, but he roused him too late;
Down fell the snow from a pitiless cloud,
And gave little squirrel a spotless white shroud.

Two little boys in a school-room were placed,
One always perfect, the other disgraced;
"Time enough yet for my learning," he said;
"I will climb, by and by, from the foot to the head."

Listen, my darling; their locks are turned gray;
One as a Governor sitteth to-day;
The other, a pauper, looks out at the door
Of the almshouse, and idles his days as of yore.

Two kinds of people we meet every day:
One is at work, the other at play,
Living uncared for, dying unknown—
The busiest hive hath ever a drone.

HOMESICK.

DOLLY knows what's the matter—Dolly and I.
It isn't the mumps nor the measles—oh! dear, I shall die!
It's the mothering we want, Dolly, the—what shall I call it?
And grandpa says he has sent—he put the 'spatch safe in his wallet.

I know well enough he dropped that telegraph 'spatch in the fire,
If mother just knew, she'd come, if 'twas on the telegraph wire!
She'd take my poor head, that is splitting this very minute,
And she'd sing "There's a Happy Land," and the hymn that has "Darling" in it.

'Course, I like grandpa's house; it's the splendidest place to stay,
When there's all the out-doors to live in, and nothing to do but play;
Somehow you forget your mother—that is, just the littlest bit,
Though if she were here, I suppose that I shouldn't mention it.

But oh! there's a difference, Dolly, when your head is so full of pains
That ('cepting the ache that's in 'em) there's nothing left of your brains.
Remember how nice it feels, Dolly, to have your head petted and "poored."
Ache? Why, I ache all over, and my bed is as hard as a board.

Nurse says "It's a sweet, lovely morning." It may be
    for all that I care;
There is just one spot in this great wide world that is
    pretty—I wish I was there!
I can see the white roses climbing all over the low porch
    door,
And the daisies and buttercups growing—I never half
    loved them before.

And mother—let's see! she's standing in that very same
    door, no doubt;
She loves to look out in the morning and see what the
    world is about,
In a pale-blue something-or-other—a loose sort of wrap-
    per, I guess;
As if a few yards of sky had been taken to make a
    dress.

And up from the pine woods yonder comes a beautiful
    woodsy smell,
And the breeze keeps a hinting of May flowers—the
    real-pink arbutus bell;
And I think most likely the robins have built in the
    cherry tree;
And by and by there'll be birdies—and I shall not be
    there to see!

Did you hear any noise, Dolly! Speak, Dolly, you lit-
    tle witch!
As if something was laughing—or crying! I couldn't
    tell which!

We've képt from crying, so far; we've choked but we
   wouldn't cry;
I've just talked it out to you, dear; I had to, or else I'd
   die.

But if that is you, mother—and I know by your lips
   that it is—
I'll just squeeze your head off!—you think that all I
   want is a kiss!
O mother! to papa and Tom you needn't go mention it,
But you know it was homesickness almost killed your
   poor little Kit!

WAR INEVITABLE.

SIR, we shall not fight our battles alone. There is a
just God who presides over the destinies of nations,
and who will raise up friends to fight our battles for us.
The battle, sir, is not to the strong alone; it is to the
vigilant, the active, the brave. Besides, sir, we have no
election. If we were base enough to desire it, it is now
too late to retire from the contest. There is no retreat
but in submission and slavery! Our chains are forged!
Their clanking may be heard on the plains of Boston!
The war is inevitable: and let it come! I repeat it, sir,
let it come!

It is in vain, sir, to extenuate the matter. Gentlemen
may cry, Peace, peace; but there is no peace. The war
is actually begun! The next gale that sweeps from the
North will bring to our ears the clash of resounding arms!
Our brethren are already in the field! Why stand we

here idle? What is it that gentlemen wish? What would they have? Is life so dear, or peace so sweet, as to be purchased at the price of chains and slavery? Forbid it, Heaven! I know not what course others may take, but as for me, give me liberty, or give me death.

Patrick Henry.

THAT CALF.

To the yard, by the barn, came the farmer one morn,
    And, calling the cattle, he said,
While they trembled with fright: "Now which of you, last night,
    Shut the barn door while I was abed?"
    Each one of them all shook his head.

Now the little calf Spot, she was down in the lot,
    And the way the rest talked was a shame;
For no one, night before, saw her shut up the door;
    But they said that she did, all the same,
    For they always made her take the blame.

Said the horse (dapple gray), "I was not up that way
    Last night, as I now recollect;"
And the bull, passing by, tossed his horns very high,
    And said, "Let who may here object,
    I say this, that calf I suspect."

Then out spoke the cow, "It is terrible now,
    To accuse honest folks of such tricks."
Said the cock in the tree, "I'm sure 'twasn't me;"
    And the sheep all cried, "Bah! (there were six)
    Now that calf's got herself in a fix."

"Why, of course we all knew 'twas the wrong thing to
    do,"
  Said the chickens. "Of course," said the cat.
"I suppose," cried the mule, "some folks think me a
    fool,
  But I'm not quite so simple as that;
  The poor calf never knows what she's at."

Just that moment, the calf, who was always the laugh
  And the jest of the yard, came in sight.
"Did you shut my barn door?" asked the farmer once
    more.
  "I did, sir, I closed it last night,"
  Said the calf; "and I thought that was right."

Then each one shook his head. "She will catch it," they
    cried,
  "Serves her right for her meddlesome ways."
Said the farmer, "Come here, little bossy, my dear,
  You have done what I cannot repay,
  And your fortune is made from to-day.

"For a wonder, last night, I forgot the door quite,
  And if you had not shut it so neat,
All my colts had slipped in, and gone right to the bin,
  And got what they ought not to eat,
  They'd have foundered themselves upon wheat."

Then each hoof of them all began loudly to bawl,
  The very mule smiled, the cock crew:
"Little Spotty, my dear, you're a favorite here,"
  They cried, "we all said it was you,
  We were so glad to give you your due."
  And the calf answered knowingly, "Boo!"

PHŒBE CARY.

JOHNNY THE STOUT.

"HO! for a frolic!"
    Said Johnny the stout;
"There's coasting and sledding—
    I'm going out."

Scarcely had Johnny
    Plunged in the snow,
When there came a complaint
    Up from his toe:

"We're cold," said the toe,
    "I and the rest;
There's ten of us freezing,
    Standing abreast."

Then up spoke an ear;
    "My, but it's labor—
Playing in winter. Eh!
    Opposite neighbor!"

"Pooh!" said his nose,
    Angry and red;
"Who wants to tingle?
    Go home to bed!"

Eight little fingers,
    Four to a thumb,
All cried together—
    "Johnny, we're numb!"

But Johnny the stout
    Wouldn't listen a minute;
Never a snow bank
    But Johnny was in it.

Tumbling and jumping,
  Shouting with glee,
Wading the snow-drifts
  Up to his knee.

Soon he forgot them—
  Fingers and toes,
Never once thought of
  The ear and the nose.

Ah! What a frolic!
  All in a glow,
Johnny grew warmer
  Out in the snow.

Often his breathing
  Came with a joke;
"Blaze away, Johnny!
  I'll do the smoke."

"And I'll do the fire,"
  Said Johnny the bold.
"Fun is the fuel
  For driving off cold."

WHAT THE MINUTES SAY.

WE are but minutes, little things,
  Each one furnished with sixty wings,
With which we fly on our unseen track,
And not a minute ever comes back.

We are but minutes; each one bears
A little burden of joys and cares;
Take patiently the minutes of pain,
The worst of minutes cannot remain.

We are but minutes; when we bring
A few of the drops from Pleasure's spring,
Taste their sweetness while yet ye may,
It takes but a minute to fly away.

THE LITTLE BOY'S LAMENT.

OH! why must I always be washed so clean
   And scrubbed and drenched for Sunday,
When you know, very well, for you've always seen,
   That I'm dirty again on Monday?

My eyes are filled with the lathery soap,
   Which adown my ears is dripping;
And my smarting eyes I can scarcely ope,
   And my lips the suds are sipping.

It's down my neck and up my nose,
   And to choke me you seem to be trying;
That I'll shut my mouth you need not suppose,
   For how can I keep from crying?

You rub as hard as ever you can,
   And your hands are hard, to my sorrow;
No woman shall wash me when I'm a man,
   And I wish I was one to-morrow.

NATURE.

NATURE will be reported—all things are engaged in writing its history. The planet, the pebble, goes attended by its shadow. The rolling rock leaves its scratches on the mountain, the river its channels in the soil, the animal its bones in the stratum, the fern and leaf their modest epitaph in the coal. The fallen drop makes its sculpture in the sand or stone; not a footstep in the snow, or along the ground, but prints, in characters more or less lasting, a map of its march; every act of man inscribes itself in the memories of his fellows and in his own face. The air is full of sounds, the sky of tokens, the ground of memoranda and signatures, and every object is covered over with hints which speak to the intelligent.

Hugh Miller.

THE BOY AND THE FROG.

SEE the frog, the slimy, green frog,
  Dozing away on that old rotten log;
      Seriously wondering
      What caused the sundering
Of the tail that he wore when a wee pollywog.

See the boy, the freckled schoolboy,
Filled with a wicked love to annoy,
      Watching the frog
      Perched on the log
With feelings akin to tumultuous joy.

See the rock, the hard, flinty rock,
Which the freckled-faced boy at the frog doth sock,
    Conscious he's sinning,
    Yet gleefully grinning
At the likely result of its terrible shock.

See the grass, the treacherous grass,
Slip from beneath his feet! Alas!
    Into the mud
    With a dull thud
He falls, and rises a slimy mass.

Now, see the frog, the hilarious frog,
Dancing a jig on his old rotten log,
    Applying his toes
    To his broad, blunt nose,
As he laughs at the boy stuck fast in the bog.

*   *   *   *   *   *

Look at the switch, the hickory switch,
Waiting to make that schoolboy twitch.
    When his mother knows
    The state of his clothes
Won't he raise his voice to its highest pitch?

NUMBER ONE.

HOMŒOPATHIC SOUP.

TAKE a robin's leg
   (Mind, the drumstick merely),
Put it in a tub
   Fill'd with water nearly;
Set it out-of-doors,
   In a place that's shady,
Let it stand a week,—
   (Three days for a lady).

Drop a spoonful of it
   In a five-pail kettle,
Which may be made of tin
   Or any baser metal;
Fill the kettle up,
   Set it on a boiling,
Strain the liquor well
   To prevent its oiling.

One atom add of salt,
   For the thickening one rice kernel,
And use to light the fire
   "The Homœopathic Journal."
Let the liquor boil
   Half-an-hour, no longer.
If 'tis for a man
   Of course you'll make it stronger.

Should you now desire
   That the soup be flavory,
Stir it once around
   With a stalk of savory.

When the broth is made,
    Nothing can excel it;
Then three times a day
    Let the patient smell it.
If he chance to die,
    Say 'twas Nature did it;
If he chance to live,
    Give the soup the credit.

LINES TO KATE.

THERE'S something in the name of Kate,
    Which many will condemn;
But listen now while I relate
    The trials of some of them.

There's advo-Kate, a charming miss;
    Could you her hand obtain,
She'll lead you in the path of bliss,
    Nor plead your cause in vain.

There's deli-Kate, a modest dame,
    And worthy of your love;
She's nice and beautiful in frame,
    As gentle as a dove.

Communi-Kate's intelligent,
    As we may well suppose;
Her fruitful mind is ever bent
    On telling what she knows.

There's intri-Kate; she's so obscure
    'Tis hard to find her out,
For she is often very sure
    To put your wits to rout.

Prevari-Kate's a stubborn mind,
   She's sure to have her way;
The cavilling, contrary jade
   Objects to all you say.

There's alter-Kate, a perfect pest,
   Much given to dispute;
Her prattling tongue can never rest;
   You cannot her refute.

There's dislo-Kate, quite in a fret,
   Who fails to gain her point;
Her case is quite unfortunate,
   And sorely out of joint.

Equivo-Kate no one will woo,
   The thing would be absurd;
She is faithless and untrue,
   You cannot take her word.

There's vindi-Kate; she's good and true,
   And strives with all her might
Her duty faithfully to do,
   And battles for the right.

There's rusti-Kate, a country lass,
   Quite fond of rural scenes;
She likes to ramble through the grass,
   And through the evergreens.

Of all the maidens you can find,
   There's none like edu-Kate;
Because she elevates the mind,
   And aims for something great.

GRAND SCHEME OF EMIGRATION.

THE Brewers should to Malt-a go,
    The Loggerheads to Scilly,
The Quakers to the Friendly Isles,
    The Furriers all to Chili.

The little squalling, brawling brats,
    That break our nightly rest,
Should be packed off to Baby-lon,
    To Lap-land, or to Brest.

From Spit-head Cooks go o'er to Greece;
    And while the Miser waits
His passage to the Guinea coast,
    Spendthrifts are in the Straits.

Spinsters should to the Needles go,
    Wine-bibbers to Burgundy;
Gourmands should lunch at Sandwich Isles,
    Wags in the Bay of Fundy.

Musicians hasten to the Sound,
    The surpliced Priest to Rome,
While still the race of Hypocrites
    At Cant-on are at home.

Lovers should hasten to Good Hope;
    To some Cape Horn is pain;
Debtors should go to Oh-i-o,
    And Sailors to the Main-e.

Hie, Bachelors, to the United States!
    Maids to the Isle of Man;
Let Gardeners go to Botany Bay,
    And Shoeblacks to Japan.

Thus, emigrants and misplaced men
   Will no longer vex us;
And all that ar'n't provided for
   Had better go to Texas.

BRAVE AND TRUE.

WHATEVER you are, be brave, boys!
   The liar's a coward and slave, boys!
     Though clever at ruses,
     And sharp at excuses,
He's a sneaking and pitiful knave, boys

Whatever you are, be frank, boys!
'Tis better than money and rank, boys;
     Still cleave to the right,
     Be lovers of light,
Be open, above board, and frank, boys!

Whatever you are, be kind, boys!
Be gentle in manner and mind, boys;
     The man gentle in mien,
     Words, and temper, I ween,
Is the gentleman truly refined, boys!

But, whatever you are, be true, boys!
Be visible through and through, boys!
     Leave to others the shamming,
     The "greening" and "cramming,"
In fun and in earnest, be true, boys!

                  HENRY DOWNTON.

THE COBBLER.

[This selection may be rendered very effective, if the reader, following the meaning of the text, should imitate the movements of a cobbler, bending forward, stitching and fitting, sewing motion, boring a hole, sticking in pegs, and hammering with fingers.]

WANDERING up and down one day,
    I peeped into a window over the way;
And putting his needle through and through,
There sat the cobbler making a shoe.

    For the world he cares never the whisk of a broom;
    All he wants is his elbow-room,
    Rap-a-tap-tap, tick-a-tack-too,
    This is the way he makes a shoe.

Over lasts of wood, his bits of leather
He stretches and fits, then sews together;
He puts his waxed-ends through and through,
And still as he stitches, his body goes too.

    For the world he cares never the whisk of a broom;
    All he wants is his elbow-room,
    Rap-a-tap-tap, tick-a-tack-too,
    This is the way he makes a shoe.

With his little sharp awl he makes a hole
Right through the upper and through the sole
He puts in one peg, or he puts in two,
And chuckles and laughs as he hammers them through.

    For the world he cares never the whisk of a broom;
    All he wants is his elbow-room,
    Rap-a-tap-tap, tick-a-tack-too,
    This is the way he makes a shoe.

WHAT'S THE MATTER?

I WONDER if the little birds
    That soar above my head
Are scolded all the sunny day,
    And then sent off to bed?

I almost wish I was a bird,
    And had a pair of wings;
I'd fly away from this dull place
    And all these stupid things.

There's always such a dreadful fuss
    If I do what I've a mind;
Mother looks so sorrowful,
    I half wish I were blind.

I'm sure 'tis not so very wrong
    For girls to like to play;
I don't know why they want us to
    Be studying all day.

I haven't learned my lesson yet,
    Or sewed that horrid seam;
I've broke my doll and sent my swing
    Above the highest beam.

Everything is going wrong,
    And has been all the day.
I hate to work, and seems to me
    I almost hate to play.

I wonder why I feel so cross
    When mother is so kind;
She sighs and speaks so very low
    When I don't want to mind.

I am a naughty, willful girl—
I know it all the while;
I'll run and tell dear mother so,
And then how soon she'll smile.

And if I live to see the sun
Upon another day,
I'll find my highest happiness
In a less selfish way.　　　　H. K. P.

PEACEABLE SECESSION.

SECESSION! Peaceable secession! Sir, your eyes and mine are never destined to see that miracle! The dismemberment of this vast country without convulsion! The breaking up of the fountains of the great deep without ruffling the surface! Who is so foolish— I beg everybody's pardon—as to expect to see any such thing?

Sir, he who sees these States now revolving in harmony around a common centre, and expects to see them quit their places, and fly off without convulsion, may look the next hour to see the heavenly bodies rush from their spheres and jostle against each other in the realms of space without causing the crush of the universe. There can be no such thing as peaceable secession. Peaceable secession is an utter impossibility.

Is the great Constitution under which we live, covering this whole country—is it to be thawed and melted away by secession, as the snows on the mountain melt under the influence of a vernal sun, disappear almost unobserved and run off? No, sir! No, sir! I will not state what might produce the disruption of the Union; but, sir, I see as plainly as I see the sun in heaven, what that disruption itself must produce; I see that it must produce war, and such a war as I will not describe in its twofold character.

WEBSTER.

BABY'S SOLILOQUY.

[The following selection can be made very humorous if the person reading it assumes the tones of a very little child, and in appropriate places imitates the cry of a baby.]

I AM here. And if this is what they call the world, I don't think much of it. It's a very flannelly world, and smells of paregoric awfully. It's a dreadful light world, too, and makes me blink, I tell you. And I don't know what to do with my hands; I think I'll dig my fists in my eyes. No, I won't. I'll scratch at the corner of my blanket and chew it up, and then I'll holler; whatever happens, I'll holler. And the more paregoric they give me, the louder I'll yell. That old nurse puts the spoon in the corner of my mouth, sidewise like, and keeps tasting my milk herself all the while. She spilt snuff in it last night, and when I hollered she trotted me. That comes of being a two-days-old baby. Never mind; when I'm a man, I'll pay her back good. There's a pin sticking in me now, and if I say a word about it, I'll be trotted or fed; and I would rather have catnip-tea. I'll tell you who I am. I found out to-day. I heard folks say, "Hush! don't wake up Emeline's baby; and I suppose that pretty, white-faced woman over on the pillow is Emeline.

No, I was mistaken; for a chap was in here just now and wanted to see Bob's baby; and looked at me and said I was a funny little toad, and looked just like Bob. He smelt of cigars. I wonder who else I belong to! Yes, there's another one—that's "Gamma." "It was Gamma's baby, so it was." I declare, I do not know who I belong to; but I'll holler, and maybe I'll find out. There comes snuffy with catnip-tea. I'm going to sleep. I wonder why my hands won't go where I want them to!

A TRIBUTE TO WATER.

WHERE is the liquor which God the eternal brews for all His children? Not in the simmering still, over smoky fires choked with poisonous gases, and surrounded with the stench of sickening odors and rank corruptions, doth your Father in heaven prepare the precious essence of life—the pure cold water. But in the green glade and grassy dell, where the red deer wanders, and the child loves to play, there God brews it. And down, low down in the deepest valleys, where the fountains murmur and the rills sing; and high upon the tall mountain tops, where the naked granite glitters like gold in the sun; where the storm-cloud broods, and the thunder-storms crash; and away far out on the wide, wild sea, where the hurricane howls music, and the big waves roar, the chorus sweeping the march of God: there He brews it—that beverage of life and health-giving water. And everywhere it is a thing of beauty; gleaming in the dew-drop, singing in the summer rain, shining in the ice-gem till the leaves all seemed turned to living jewels, spreading a golden veil over the setting sun, or a white gauze around the midnight moon.

Sporting in the cataract; sleeping in the glacier; dancing in the hail-shower; folding its bright snow curtains softly about the wintry world; and waving the many-colored iris, that seraph's zone of the sky, whose warp is the rain-drop of earth, whose woof is the sunbeam of heaven; all chequered over with celestial flowers by the mystic hand of refraction.

Still always it is beautiful, that life-giving water; no poison bubbles on its brink; its foam brings not madness and murder; no blood stains its liquid glass; pale widows and starving orphans weep no burning tears in its depths; no drunken shrieking ghost from the grave curses it in the words of eternal despair. Speak, my friends, would you exchange it for demon's drink, alcohol?

JOHN B. GOUGH.

GRANDPAPA'S SPECTACLES.

GRANDPAPA'S spectacles cannot be found!
    He has searched all the rooms, high and low, round and round;
Now he calls to the young ones, and what does he say!
"Ten cents" to the child who will find them to-day.

Then Harry and Nelly and Edward all ran,
And a most thorough search for the glasses began.
And dear little Nell in her generous way
Said, "I'll look for them, Grandpa, without any pay."

All through the big Bible she searched with care,
It lies on the table by Granpapa's chair.
They feel in his pockets, they peep in his hat,
They pull out the sofa and shake out the mat.

Then down on the floor, like good-natured bears,
Go Harry and Ned under tables and chairs,
Till quite out of breath, Ned is heard to declare,
He believed that those glasses are not anywhere.

But Nelly, who, leaning on Grandpapa's knee,
Was thinking most earnestly, "where can they be?"
Looked suddenly up in the kind, faded eyes,
And her own shining brown ones grew big with surprise.

She clapped with her hands, all her dimples came out,
She turned to the boys with a bright, roguish shout,
"You may leave off your looking, both Harry and Ned,
For there are the glasses on Grandpapa's head."

SIN.

USE sin as it will use you; spare it not, for it will not spare you; it is your murderer, and the murderer of the world; use it, therefore, as a murderer should be used. Kill it before it kills you; and though it kill your bodies, it shall not be able to kill your souls; and though it bring you to the grave, as it did your Head, it shall not be able to keep you there.

BAXTER.

FEBRUARY TWENTY-SECOND.

IN seventeen hundred thirty-two,
   This very month and day,
Winking and blinking at the light,
   A little baby lay.

No doubt they thought the little man
   A goodly child enough;
But time has proved that he was made
   Of most uncommon stuff.

The little babe became a man
   That everybody knew
Would finish well what he began,
   And prove both firm and true.

So when the Revolution came,
   That made our nation free,
They couldn't find a better man
   For general, you see.

As general, he never failed
   Or faltered; so they thought
He ought to be the President,
   And so I'm sure he ought.

And then he did his part so well
   As President—'twas plain
They couldn't do a better thing
   Than choose him yet again.

Through all his life they loved him well,
   And mourned him when he died;
And ever since his noble name
   Has been our nation's pride.

The lesson of his life is clear,
   And easy quite to guess,
Be firm and true, if you would make
   Your life a grand success.
Joy Allison.

THE STOLEN CUSTARD.

SUGAR-TOOTHED Dick
   For dainties was sick,
So he slyly stole into the kitchen,
   Snatched a cup from the pantry,
   And darted out quick,
Unnoticed by mother or Gretchen.

   Whispered he, "There's no cake,
   For to-morrow they bake,
But this custard looks rich and delicious;
   How they'll scold at the rats,
   Or the mice, or the cats;
For of me I don't think they're suspicious.

   "They might have filled up
   Such a mean little cup!
And for want of a spoon I must drink it:
   But 'tis easy to pour—
   Hark! who's at the door?"
And the custard went down ere you'd think it.

   With a shriek he sprang up;
   To the floor dashed the cup;
Then he howled, tumbled, sputtered, and blustered,
   Till the terrible din
   Brought the whole household in—
He had swallowed a cupful of mustard!

SOMEBODY'S MOTHER.

THE woman was old, and ragged, and gray,
And bent with the chill of a winter's day;
The streets were white with a recent snow,
And the woman's feet with age were slow.

At the crowded crossing she waited long,
Jostled aside by the careless throng
Of human beings who passed her by,
Unheeding the glance of her anxious eye.

Down the street with laughter and shout,
Clad in the freedom of "school let out,"
Come happy boys, like a flock of sheep,
Hailing the snow piled white and deep;
Past the woman, so old and gray,
Hastened the children on their way.

None offered a helping hand to her,
So weak and timid, afraid to stir,
Lest the carriage wheels or the horses' feet
Should trample her down in the slippery street.

At last came out of the merry troop
The gayest boy of all the group;
He paused beside her, and whispered low,
"I'll help you across, if you wish to go."

Her aged hand on his strong young arm
She placed, and so without hurt or harm,
He guided the trembling feet along,
Proud that his own were young and strong;
Then back again to his friends he went,
His young heart happy and well content.

"She's somebody's mother, boys, you know,
For all she's aged, and poor, and slow;
And some one, some time, may lend a hand
To help my mother—you understand?—
If ever she's poor, and old, and gray,
And her own dear boy so far away."

"Somebody's mother" bowed low her head,
In her home that night, and the prayer she said
Was: "God, be kind to that noble boy,
Who is somebody's son, and pride, and joy."

Faint was the voice, and worn and weak,
But the Father hears when His children speak;
Angels caught the faltering word,
And "Somebody's Mother's" prayer was heard.
                                    MACMILLAN.

WILLIE'S BREECHES.

I'M just a little boy, you know,
   And hardly can remember,
When people ask how old I am,
   To tell 'em four last 'vember.
And yet for all I am so small,
   I made so many stitches
For mamma's fingers, that she put
   Her little boy in breeches.

You may be sure that I was glad;
   I marched right up and kissed her,
Then gave my bibs and petticoats,
   And all, to baby sister.

I never whine, now I'm so fine,
   And don't get into messes;
For mamma says, if I am bad,
   She'll put me back in dresses!

There's buttons up and down my legs,
   And buttons on my jacket;
I'd count 'em all, but baby makes
   Just now, an awful racket.
She's sitting there, behind the chair,
   With blocks, and dolls, and kitty,
A playing "go to gran'ma's house,"
   Alone, 'n that's a pity.

I think I'll go and help her some,
   I'm sure it would amuse me;
So I won't bother any more
   To talk—if you'll excuse me.
But first I'll stand before the glass,
   From top to toe it reaches:
Now look! there's head, and hands, and feet,
   But all the rest is breeches!

                ETTA G. SALSBURY.

WORK.

THERE is a perennial nobleness, and even sacredness, in work. Were he ever so benighted, or forgetful of his high calling, there is always hope in a man that actually and earnestly works; in idleness alone there is perpetual despair. Consider how, even in the meanest sorts of labor, the whole soul of a man is composed into real harmony. He bends himself with free valor against his task; and doubt, desire, sorrow, remorse, indignation, despair itself, shrink murmuring far off in their caves. The glow of labor in him is a purifying fire, wherein all poison is burned up; and of smoke itself there is made a bright and blessed flame.

Blessed is he who has found his work; let him ask no other blessedness; he has a life purpose. Labor is life. From the heart of the worker rises the celestial force, breathed into him by Almighty God, awakening him to all nobleness, to all knowledge. Hast thou valued patience, courage, openness to light, or readiness to own thy mistakes? In wrestling with the dim brute powers of fact thou wilt continually learn. For every noble work the possibilities are diffused through immensity, undiscoverable, except to faith.

Man, son of heaven! is there not in thine inmost heart a spirit of active method, giving thee no rest till thou unfold it? Complain not. Look up. See thy fellow-workmen surviving through eternity, the sacred band of immortals.

THOMAS CARLYLE.

LOVELINESS.

ONCE I knew a little girl,
    Very plain;
You might try her hair to curl
    All in vain;
On her cheek no tint of rose
Paled and blushed, or sought repose;
    She was plain.

But the thoughts that through her brain
    Came and went,
As a recompense for pain,
    Angels sent;
So full many a beauteous thing,
In her young soul blossoming,
    Gave content.

Every thought was full of grace,
    Pure and true,
And in time the homely face
    Lovelier grew;
With a heavenly radiance bright,
From the soul's reflected light
    Shining through.

So I tell you, little child,
    Plain or poor,
If your thoughts are undefiled,
    You are sure
Of the loveliness of worth;
And this beauty not of earth
    Will endure.

                MARIA LACEY.

BEING A BOY.

ONE of the best things in the world to be is a boy; it requires no experience, though it needs some practice to be a good one. The disadvantage of the position is that he does not last long enough. It is soon over. Just as you get used to being a boy, you have to be something else, with a good deal more work to do and not half so much fun. And yet every boy is anxious to be a man, and is very uneasy with the restrictions that are put upon him as a boy. There are so many bright spots in the life of a farm boy that I sometimes think I should like to live the life over again. I should almost be willing to be a girl if it were not for the chores. There is a great comfort to a boy in the amount of work he can get rid of doing. It is sometimes astonishing how slow he can go on an errand. Perhaps he couldn't explain, himself, why, when he is sent to the neighbor's after yeast, he stops to stone the frogs. He is not exactly cruel, but he wants to see if he can hit 'em. It is a curious fact about boys, that two will be a great deal slower in doing anything than one. Boys have a great power of helping each other do nothing. But say what you will about the general usefulness of boys, a farm without a boy would very soon come to grief. He is always in demand. In the first place, he is to do all the errands, go to the store, the post-office, and to carry all sorts of messages. He would like to have as many legs as a wheel has spokes, and rotate about in the same way. This he sometimes tries to do, and people who have seen him "turning cart-wheels" along the side of the road have supposed he was amusing himself and idling his time. He was only trying to invent a new mode of locomotion, so that he could economize his legs and do his errands with greater dispatch. Leap-frog is one of his methods of getting over the ground quickly. He has a natural genius for combining pleasure with business.

CHARLES DUDLEY WARNER.

WE MUST ALL SCRATCH.

SAID the first little chicken,
  With a queer little squirm,
"I wish I could find
  A fat little worm."

Said the next little chicken,
  With an odd little shrug,
"I wish I could find
  A fat little bug."

Said the third little chicken,
  With a sharp little squeal,
"I wish I could find
  Some nice yellow meal."

Said the fourth little chicken,
  With a small sigh of grief,
"I wish I could find
  A green little leaf."

Said the fifth little chicken,
  With a faint little moan,
"I wish I could find
  A wee gravel stone."

"Now, see here," said the mother,
  From the green garden patch,
"If you want any breakfast,
  Just come here and scratch."

BLOWING BUBBLES.

WHERE the grass had been newly mown,
Before a rustic cottage home,
An idle schoolboy strolled away,
To waste his time in childish play.

The school-bell rang, but there stood he,
Happy as ever boy could be,
Free from books, and schoolboy troubles,
With grandpa's pipe, blowing bubbles.

Away went bubbles, thick and fast,
Like sparks from out a furnace blast,
His eyes as large as saucers grew,
As higher up the bubbles flew.

With outstretched mouth and beaming eyes,
He watched them, mounting toward the skies,
And shook all over with delight,
To see them vanish out of sight.

While Conrad thus his time employed,
His grandpapa was much annoyed;
When from a nap he soon awoke,
And rose to take his wonted smoke.

He seized his stout "Old Hickory" cane,
Went quick to where his pipe had lain,
But looked the picture of despair,
To find the pipe no longer there.

In every nook and corner then,
Through all the rooms, where he had been,
He went to work with vigorous mind,
Its secret hiding-place to find.

He put his glasses on his nose,
Old-fashioned "specs" with iron bows,
Then turned about, and looked again,
Where he had looked before in vain.

But when his pipe could not be found,
His groans were heard the house around,
While, sad to tell, his pet grandchild
Was blowing bubbles all this while.

That good old face, superbly hale,
Suddenly turned to ghastly pale;
He staggered back upon his bed,
Where Conrad came, and found him dead.

The doctors all at once agreed
That he had died (if dead indeed)
From causes to themselves unknown,
"Unless the want of smoke alone."

In yonder church-yard, down the lane,
A tombstone stands, with grandpa's name,
Where all old smokers well can see
How sad a fate their own may be.

That marble shaft, erect and trim,
Bears on its side Death's face so grim,
With broken pipe carved underneath,
And these few words "in bass-relief:"

"For want of smoke, this old man died,
Of all things else he had enough;
His good wife rests here by his side,
Who died of using too much snuff."

     Rev. O. F. Starkey.

WHEN THE FROST IS ON THE PUNKIN.

WHEN the frost is on the punkin and the fodder's in the shock,
And you hear the kyouck and gobble of the struttin' turkey cock,
And the clackin' of the guineys and the cluckin' of the hens,
And the rooster's hallylooyer, as he tiptoes on the fence,
Oh! it's then the time a feller is a feelin' at his best,
With the risin' sun to greet him from a night of gracious rest,
As he leaves the house bareheaded, and goes out to feed the stock,
When the frost is on the punkin and the fodder's in the shock.

They's somepin kind o' heartylike about the atmosphere
When the heat of summer's over and the coolin' fall is here—
Of course we miss the flowers and the blossoms on the trees,
And the mumble of the hummin' birds, and buzzin' of the bees;

But the air's so appetizin', and the landscape through
  the haze
Of a crisp and sunny morning of the early autumn days
Is a picture that no painter has the colorin' to mock—
When the frost is on the punkin and the fodder's in the
  shock.

The husky, rusty rustle of the tossels of the corn,
And the raspin' of the tangled leaves, as golden as the
  morn ;
The stubble in the furries, kind o' lonesome like, but
  still
A preachin' sermons to us of the barns they growed to
  fill ;
The strawstack in the medder and the reaper in the
  shed ;
The hosses in the stalls below, the clover overhead ;
Oh ! it sets my heart a clickin', like the tickin' of a clock,
When the frost is on the punkin and the fodder's in the
  shock !

AMERICA'S OBLIGATIONS TO ENGLAND.

THE honorable gentleman has asked : " And now, will these Americans, children planted by our care, nourished up by our indulgence and protected by our arms—will they grudge to contribute their mite ?"

They planted by your care? No, your oppressions planted them in America ! They fled from your tyranny to a then uncultivated and inhospitable country. There they exposed themselves to almost all the hardships to which human nature is liable.

They nourished up by your indulgence? They grew by your neglect of them. As soon as you began to care about them, that care was exercised in sending persons to rule them, to spy out their liberties, to misrepresent their actions, to prey upon their substance.

They protected by your arms? They have nobly taken up arms in your defense—have exerted their valor for your own emolument. And believe me—remember I this day told you so—that same spirit of freedom which actuated these Americans at first will accompany them still. They are now as truly loyal as any subjects the King has, but they are a people jealous of their liberties, and a people who will vindicate those liberties to the last drop of their blood.

Colonel Barre.

PLANTING HIMSELF TO GROW.

DEAR little, bright-eyed Willie,
   Always so full of glee,
Always so very mischievous,
   The pride of our home is he.

One bright summer day we found him
   Close by the garden wall,
Standing so grave and dignified
   Beside a sunflower tall.

His tiny feet he had covered
   With the moist and cooling sand;
The stalk of the great, tall sunflower
   He grasped with his chubby hand.

When he saw us standing near him,
Gazing so wonderingly
At his babyship, he greeted us
With a merry shout of glee.

We asked our darling what pleased him;
He replied, with a face aglow,
"Mamma, I'm going to be a man;
I've planted myself to grow."

DIGNITY IN LABOR.

IN the search after true dignity, you may point me to the sceptred prince, ruling over mighty empires, to the lord of broad acres teeming with fertility, or the owner of coffers bursting with gold; you may tell me of them or of learning, of the historian or of the philosopher, the poet or the artist, and, while prompt to render such men all the honor which in varying degrees may be their due, I would emphatically declare that neither power nor nobility, nor wealth, nor learning, nor genius, nor benevolence, nor all combined, have a monopoly of dignity. I would take you to the dingy office, where day by day the pen plies its weary task; or to the shop, where from early morning till half the world have sunk to sleep, the necessities and luxuries of life are distributed, with scarce an interval for food, and none for thought; I would descend farther, I would take you to the plowman, plodding along his furrows; to the mechanic, throwing the swift shuttle or tending the busy wheels; to the miner, groping his darksome way in the deep caverns of earth; to the man of the trowel, the hammer, or the forge, and if, while he diligently prosecutes his humble toil, he looks up with a brave heart and loving eye to heaven—if in what he does he recognizes his God, and expects his wages from on high—if, while thus laboring on earth, he anticipates the rest of heaven, and can say, as did a poor man once, who, when pitied on account of humble lot, said, taking off his hat, "Sir, I am the son of a King, I am a child of God, and when I die, angels will carry me from this Union Workhouse direct to the Court of Heaven." Then, having shown you such a spectacle, may I not ask—Is there not dignity in labor?

NEWMAN HALL.

WHERE DID YOU COME FROM, BABY?

"WHERE did you come from, baby dear?"
"Out of the every-where into the here."
"Where did you get your eyes so blue?"
"Out of the sky as I came through."

"What makes the light in them sparkle and spin?"
"Some of the starry spikes left in."
"Where did you get that little tear?"
"I found it waiting when I got here."

"What makes your forehead so smooth and high?"
"A soft hand stroked it as I went by."
"What makes your cheek like a warm white rose?"
"Something better than any one knows."

"Whence that three-cornered smile of bliss?"
"Three angels gave me at once a kiss."
"Where did you get that pearly ear?"
"God spoke, and it came out to hear."

"Where did you get those arms and hands?"
"Love made itself into hooks and bands."
"Feet, whence did you come, you darling things?"
"From the same body as the cherubs' wings."

"How did they all just come to be you?"
"God thought about me, and so I grew."
"But how did you come to us, my dear?"
"God thought of you, and so I am here."
GEORGE MACDONALD.

A LITTLE BOY'S TROUBLES.

I THOUGHT when I'd learned my letters
   That all of my troubles were done;
But I find myself much mistaken—
   They only have just begun.
Learning to read was awful,
   But nothing like learning to write;
I'd be sorry to have you tell it,
   But my copy-book is a sight!

The ink gets over my fingers;
   The pen cuts all sorts of shines,
And won't do at all as I bid it;
   The letters won't stay on the lines,

But go up and down and all over,
   As though they were dancing a jig—
They are there in all shapes and sizes,
   Medium, little, and big.

The tails of the g's are so contrary,
   The handles get on the wrong side
Of the d's, and the k's, and the h's,
   Though I've certainly tried and tried
To make them just right; it is dreadful,
   I really don't know what to do,
I'm getting almost distracted —
   My teacher says she is too.

There'd be some comfort in learning
   If one could get through: instead
Of that there are books awaiting
   Quite enough to craze my head.
There's the multiplication table,
   And grammar, and—oh! dear me,
There's no good place for stopping
   When one has begun, I see.

My teacher says, little by little
   To the mountain tops we climb;
It isn't all done in a minute,
   But only a step at a time;
She says that all the scholars,
   All the wise and learned men,
Had each to begin as I do;
   If that's so, where's my pen?

CARLOTTA PERRY.

NOTES FROM A BATTLE-FIELD.

THE farmer and the farmer's wife
   A setting hen defied,
And for awhile glad vict'ry seemed
   To crown the aggressor's side.

The coach-house was the battle-field,
   And Biddy's will was firm,
Within its sacred precincts there
   To serve her little term.

What though they shut the woodshed door,
   And showed her there a nest—
Filled to the very brim with eggs—
   To soothe her ruffled breast.

This Biddy knew a thing or two,
   And, from a window high,
Back to her chosen nest again
   Triumphantly did fly!

'Twas shoo! here, and shoo! there,
   And shriek, and squawk, and flutter,
Until that peaceful farm was filled
   With noises just too utter!

The angry farmer lost his wits,
   The wife her apron shook,
And all because this setting hen
   Had such determined look.

They poked her, they punched her;
   They breathed in accents dire;
But yet that fussy feathered fowl
   Her purpose kept entire.

And even though a wagon-pole
  Was brandished at a pinch,
They could not scare nor terrify
  Nor budge that hen an inch.

At last the farmer charged the hen,
  But punched a mild-eyed cow,
Who poked the horse, who kicked the pig,
  Who raised a dreadful row.

The pig broke out and found his way
  Down to the garden bed,
And followed on his martial heels
  The horse with frantic tread.

They visited the rows of beets,
  The hills of early corn,
The hot-beds and the lettuce-beds,
  And left them all forlorn.

And all that day, and all next week,
  The farmer did repair;
His woodshed door is fastened still,
  But Biddy is not there.

Look for her in the carriage-house,
  Where, prickly as a thistle,
That setting hen is sitting yet,
  In one perpetual bristle.

The farmer and the farmer's wife
  At last have had to yield,
And Biddy sits victorious
  Upon that battle-field.

O fickle goddess Victory!
  To thus desert us men,
And give the plume of conqueror
  To keeping of a hen!

Dear me! what are we coming to,
  To thus disgrace our sires?
What shall we tell posterity
  If any one inquires?

S. C. STONE.

THREE GOOD DOCTORS.

THE best of all the pill-box crew
  Since ever time began,
Are the doctors who have most to do
  With the health of a hearty man.

And so I count them up again,
  And praise them as I can;
There's Dr. Diet, and Dr. Quiet,
  And Dr. Merryman.

There's Dr. Diet, he tries my tongue,
  "I know you well," says he;
"Your stomach is poor, and your liver is sprung,
  We must make your food agree."

And Dr. Quiet, he feels my wrist,
  And he gravely shakes his head,
"Now, now, dear sir, I must insist
  That you go at ten to bed."

But Dr. Merryman for me,
  Of all the pill-box crew!
For he smiles and says, as he fobs his fee,
  "Laugh on, whatever you do!"

So now I eat what I ought to eat,
  And at ten I go to bed,
And I laugh in the face of cold or heat;
  For thus have the doctors said!

And so I count them up again,
  And praise them as I can;
There's Dr. Diet, and Dr. Quiet,
  And Dr. Merryman.
S. W. DUFFIELD, D. D

ON CONQUERING AMERICA.

YOU cannot, I venture to say, you cannot conquer America. Your armies in the last war effected everything that could be effected, and what was it? What is your present situation? We do not know the worst, but we know that in seven campaigns we have done nothing and suffered much.

As to conquest, therefore, I repeat it, that is impossible. You may swell every effort and every expense still more extravagantly; pile and accumulate every assistance you can buy or borrow; traffic and barter with every little pitiful German prince that sells and sends his subjects to the shambles of a foreign country: your efforts are forever impotent and vain.

They are doubly impotent and vain from this mercenary aid on which you rely; for it irritates, to an incurable resentment, the minds of your enemies to overrun them with the sordid sons of rapine and of plunder, devoting them and their possessions to the rapacity of hireling cruelty.

If I were an American, as I am an Englishman, while a foreign troop was landed in my country, I never would lay down my arms—never! never! never!

LORD CHATHAM.

THE INDIAN BRAVE.

I AM fresh from the conflict—I'm drunk with the blood
   Of the white men, who chased me o'er prairie and
      flood,
Till I trapped them at last, and exultingly swore
That my fearless red warriors should revel in gore!
I have well kept my oath, O Manitou, the Just!
Three hundred white hirelings are low in the dust.
The unequal conflict was bloody and brief,
And they weep for their men and their golden-haired
      chief.

I hate the palefaces! I'll fight to the death
While the prairies are mine, and a warrior has breath!
By the bones of our fathers, whose ruin they wrought,
When they first trod our land, and for sympathy
      sought—
By the souls of our slain, when our villages burned—
By all the black vices our people have learned,
No season of rest shall my enemies see,
Till the earth drinks my blood, or my people are free

FRANCIS S. SMITH

JOHNNY'S POCKET.

Do you know what's in my pottet?
　　Such a lot o' treasures in it!
　Listen, now, while I bedin it;
　Such a lot o' sings it hold,
　　And all there is you sall be told—
Everysin' dat's in my pottet,
And when, and where, and how I dot it.

First of all, here's in my pottet
　　A beauty shell; I picked it up;
　And here's the handle of a cup
　That somebody has broke at tea;
　　The shell's a hole in it, you see;
Nobody knows that I have dot it,
I keep it safe here in my pottet.

And here's my ball, too, in my pottet,
　　And here's my pennies, one, two, three,
　That Aunt Mary gave to me;
　To-morrow day I'll buy a spade,
　　When I'm out walking with the maid.
I can't put dat here in my pottet,
But I can use it when I've dot it.

Here's some more sin's in my pottet;
　　Here's my lead, and here's my string,
　And once I had an iron ring,
　But through a hole it lost one day;
　　And here is what I always say—
A hole's the worst sin in a pottet—
Have it mended when you've dot it.

SIX O'CLOCK P. M.

THE workshops open wide their doors
    At six o'clock P. M.,
And workmen issue forth by scores
    At six o'clock P. M.
Of all the minutes in array,
Or hours that go to make the day,
There's none so welcome, so they say,
    As six o'clock P. M.

How many children show delight
    At six o'clock P. M.,
How many homes are rendered bright
    At six o'clock P. M.
How many little happy feet
Go out into the busy street,
With joyous bounds papa to meet,
    At six o'clock P. M.

Thousands of tables draped in white
    At six o'clock P. M.,
The gathered families invite
    At six o'clock P. M.
And as they eat the frugal fare,
They quite forget their toil and care,
And drop their heavy burdens there,
    At six o'clock P. M.

Then blow, ye shrieking whistles, blow!
    At six o'clock P. M.,
Ring out, releasing bells, ring out!
And bid the welkin take the shout,
And echo it all round about,
    "'Tis six o'clock P. M."

A SOLLUM FAC'.

A WERRY funny feller is de ole plantation mule;
An' nobody'll play wid him unless he is a fool.
De bestest ting to do w'en you meditates about him,
Is to kinder sorter calkerlate you'll get along widout him.

W'en you try to 'proach dat mule from de front endwise,
He look as meek as Moses, but his looks is full ob lies;
He doesn't move a muscle, he doesn't even wink;
An' you say his dispersition's better'n people tink.

He stan' so still you s'pose he is a monument of grace;
An' you almos' see a 'nevolent expression on his face;
But dat 'nevolent expression is de mask dat's allers worn;
For ole Satan is behin' it jest as sure as you is born.

Den you cosset him a little, an' you pat his other end,
An' you has a reverlation dat he aint so much your friend;
You has made a big mistake; but before de heart repents,
You is histed werry sudden to de odder side de fence.

Well, you feel like you'd been standin' on de locomotive track
An' de engine come an' hit you in de middle ob de back;
You don' know wat has happened, you can scarcely cotch your breff;
But you tink you've made de 'quaintance ob a werry vi'lent deff.

Now a sin in de soul is percisely like de mule;
An' nobody'll play wid it, unless he is a fool.
It looks so mitey innercent; but honey, dear, beware!
For although de kick is hidden, de kick is allers there.

THE LITTLE LIGHT.

THE light shone dim on the headland,
    For the storm was raging high;
I shaded my eyes from the inner glare,
    And gazed on the west, gray sky.
It was dark and lowering; on the sea
    The waves were booming loud,
And the snow and the piercing winter sleet
    Wove over all a shroud.

"God pity the men on the sea to-night!"
    I said to my little ones,
And we shuddered as we heard afar
    The sound of minute-guns.
My good man came in, in his fishing coat
    (He was wet and cold that night),
And he said, "There'll lots of ships go down
    On the headland rocks to-night."

"Let the lamp burn all night, mother,"
    Cried little Mary then;
"'Tis but a little light, but still
    It might save drowning men."
Oh! nonsense!" cried her father (he
    Was tired and cross that night),
"The headland lighthouse is enough."
    And he put out the light.

That night, on the rocks below us,
    A noble ship went down,
But one was saved from the ghastly wreck,
    The rest were left to drown.

"We steered by a little light," he said,
  "Till we saw it sink from view;
If they'd only 'a left that light all night
  My mates might have been here, too!"

Then little Mary sobbed aloud;
  Her father blushed for shame;
"'Twas our light that you saw," he said,
  "And I'm the one to blame."
'Twas a little light—how small a thing!
  And trifling was its cost,
Yet for want of it a ship went down,
  And a hundred souls were lost.

THE BIRD AND THE BABY.

WHAT does little birdie say
  In her nest at peep of day?
Let me fly, says little birdie,
Mother, let me fly away.
Birdie, rest a little longer,
Till the little wings are stronger.
So it rests a little longer,
Then it flies away.

What does little baby say
In her bed at peep of day?
Baby says, like little birdie,
Let me rise and fly away.
Baby, sleep a little longer,
Till the little wings are stronger.
If she sleeps a little longer,
  Baby too shall fly away.

ALFRED TENNYSON.

THE RETURN FROM BATTLE.

Io! they come, they come! garlands for every shrine!
Strike lyres to greet them home! bring roses, pour
ye wine!
Swell, swell the Dorian lute through the blue, triumphant sky!
Let the cittern's tone salute the sons of victory.
With the offering of bright blood they have ransomed
hearth and tomb,
Vineyard, and field, and flood. Io! they come, they
come!

Sing it where olives wave, and by the glittering sea,
And o'er each hero's grave, sing, sing, the land is free!
Mark ye the flashing oars, and the spears that light the
deep!
How the festal sunshine pours where the lords of battle
sweep!
Each hath brought back his shield; maid, greet thy
lover home!
Mother, from that proud field, Io! thy son is come!

Who murmured of the dead? Hush, boding voice!
We know
That many a shining head lies in its glory low.
Breathe not those names to-day! They shall have their
praise ere long,
With a power all hearts to sway, in ever-burning song.
But now shed flowers, pour wine, to hail the conquerors
home;
Bring wreaths for every shrine. Io! they come, they
come!

THE AMERICAN FLAG.

THE flag of the Union—what precious associations cluster around it! Not only have our fathers set up this banner in the name of God over the well-won battle-fields of the Revolution, and over the cities and towns which they rescued from despotic rule; but think where their descendants have carried it and raised it in conquest or protection!

Through what clouds of dust and smoke has it passed—what storms of shot and shell—what scenes of fire and blood! Not only at Saratoga, at Monmouth, and at Yorktown, but at Lundy's Lane and New Orleans, at Buena Vista and Chapultepec.

It is the same glorious old flag which, inscribed with the dying words of Lawrence, "Don't give up the ship," was hoisted on Lake Erie by Commodore Perry, just on the eve of his great naval victory,—the same old flag which our great chieftain bore in triumph to the proud city of the Aztecs, and planted upon the heights of her national palaces.

Brave hands raised it above the eternal regions of ice in the Arctic seas, and have set it up on the summits of the lofty mountains of the distant West. Where has it not gone, the pride of its friends and the terror of its foes? What countries and seas has it not visited? Where has not the American citizen been able to stand beneath its guardian folds and defy the world?

With what joy and exultation have seamen and tourists gazed upon its stars and stripes, read in it the history of their nation's glory, received from it the full sense of security, and drawn from it the inspiration of patriotism! How many have lived for it, and how many have died for it! How many heroes have its folds covered in death!

And wherever that flag has gone it has been a herald of a better day—it has been the pledge of freedom, of justice, of order, of civilization, and of Christianity. Tyrants only have hated it. All who sigh for the triumph of righteousness and truth salute and love it.

A. P. PUTNAM.

LOST TOMMY.

PRAY, have you seen our Tommy?
  He's the cutest little fellow,
With cheeks as round as apples,
  And hair the softest yellow.
You see, 'twas quite a while ago,—
  An hour or two, perhaps,—
When grandma sent him off to buy
  A pound of ginger-snaps.

We have traced him to the baker's,
  And part way back again;
We found a little paper sack
  Lying empty in the lane.
But Tommy and the ginger-snaps
  Are missing totally;
I hope they both will reappear
  In time enough for tea.

We have climbed up to the garret,
  And scoured the cellar through;
We have ransacked every closet,
  And the barn and orchard too;

We have hunted through the kitchen,
    And the pantry? Oh! of course,—
We have screamed and shouted "Tommy"
    Until we're fairly hoarse.

Poor mamma goes distracted,
    And pretty Auntie May
Is sure the darling cherub
    Has somehow lost his way.
Well, well, I'll give another look
    Into the nursery;
I hardly think the little rogue
    Can hide away from me.

Ah! here's the laundry basket,
    Within I'll take a peep.
Why—what is this curled up so tight?
    'Tis Tommy, fast asleep.
O mamma, auntie, grandma!
    Come and see the fun.
Tommy, where's the ginger-snaps?
    "Eaten!—every one!"

"Bless my heart!" laughs auntie;
    "Dear, dear, I shall collapse;
Where could he stow them all away?
    A pound of ginger-snaps!"

But mamma falls to kissing,
    Forgetting fright and toil,
While grandma bustles out to fetch
    A dose of castor oil.

                Mrs. Julia M. Dana.

THE FOOLISH HAREBELL.

A HAREBELL hung its willful head:
"I am tired, so tired! I wish I was dead."

She hung her head in the mossy dell:
"If all were over, then all were well."

The wind he heard, and was pitiful;
He waved her about to make her cool.

"Wind, you are rough," said the dainty bell;
"Leave me alone—I am not well."

And the wind, at the voice of the drooping dame,
Sank in his heart, and ceased for shame.

"I am hot, so hot!" she sighed and said;
"I am withering up; I wish I was dead."

Then the sun, he pitied her pitiful case,
And drew a thick veil over his face.

"Cloud, go away, and don't be rude;
I am not—I don't see why you should."

The cloud withdrew, and the harebell cried,
"I am faint, so faint! and no water beside!"

And the dew came down its million-fold path;
But she murmured, "I did not want a bath."

A boy came by in the morning gray;
He plucked the harebell, and threw it away.

The harebell shivered, and cried, "Oh! oh!
I am faint, so faint! Come, dear wind, blow."

The wind blew softly, and did not speak.
She thanked him kindly, but grew more weak.

"Sun, dear sun, I am cold," she said.
He rose; but lower she drooped her head.

"O rain! I am withering; all the blue
Is fading out of me;—come, please do."

The rain came down as fast as it could,
But for all its will, it did her no good.

She shuddered and shriveled, and moaning said;
"Thank you all kindly;" and then she was dead.

Let us hope, let us hope, when she comes next year,
She'll be simple and sweet. But I fear, I fear.
GEORGE MACDONALD.

ONLY A BABY SMALL.

ONLY a baby small, dropped from the skies;
Only a laughing face, two sunny eyes;
Only two cherry lips, one chubby nose;
Only two little hands, ten little toes;
Only a golden head, curly and soft;
Only a tongue that wags loudly and oft;
Only a little brain, unvexed by thought;
Only a little heart, troubled by naught;
Only a tender flower, sent us to rear;
Only a life to love while we are here.
MATTHIAS BARR.

BRUTUS ON THE DEATH OF CÆSAR.

ROMANS, countrymen, and lovers! Hear me for my cause, and be silent that you may hear. Believe me for mine honor; and have respect to mine honor that you may believe. Censure me in your wisdom, and awake your senses that you may the better judge.

If there be any in this assembly, any dear friend of Cæsar's, to him I say that Brutus' love to Cæsar was not less than his. If, then, that friend demand why Brutus rose against Cæsar, this is my answer: Not that I loved Cæsar less, but that I loved Rome more. Had you rather Cæsar were living, and die all slaves, than that Cæsar were dead, to live all freemen?

As Cæsar loved me, I weep for him; as he was fortunate, I rejoice at it; as he was valiant, I honor him; but as he was ambitious, I slew him! There are tears for his love; joy for his fortune; honor for his valor; and death for his ambition!

SHAKESPEARE.

MISCELLANEOUS.

THREE LITTLE MUSHROOMS.

[A performance for three very little girls. They should be dressed in white, cream color, or pale pink—each carrying an open parasol directly over the head, to imitate a mushroom top. The parasols should be covered with the same material as that of which the dresses are made.]

FIRST GIRL.

Three little toad-stools,
   Don't you see?
Jes' as tunnin' as
   We can be.

SECOND GIRL.

Where did we come from?
   We don't know,
Guess in the same place
   Violets grow.

THIRD GIRL.

What are we dood for?
   Jes' to keep
Rain from the mosses
   When they sleep.

FIRST GIRL.

What else dood for?
   Lem' me see!
Fool boys, sometimes,
   'Tween you an' me.

SECOND GIRL.

How old are we?
   Don't know, quite—
Reckon we came in
   A shower last night.

THIRD GIRL.

Where are we goin' to.
   Oh! now, say!
Wif all de flowers
   In mamma's bouquet.

REAL ELOCUTION.

[This can be made a most laughable affair. Five boys ranging from fourteen to sixteen years of age should be selected—such as can act well and who can make the by-play full of amusing incidents. There must be an air of reality imparted to the whole, or the performers will fail in producing the best effect. The tallest boy may represent the Professor, and he should speak in a full, deep tone, and bear himself in a very pompous manner.]

Professor (entering and followed by four or five boys).—Now, young gentlemen, we have met to learn the wonderful art of elocution. This word is derived from two Latin words, e, out of, and loquor, loqui, locutus, to speak, so the word means to speak out. Half the world speak down their throats—that is not elocution. I differ from every other teacher in this. I do everything called for in the piece. If a cough is mentioned, why, I stop and cough; if a horse is spoken of, then I whinny like a horse. This I call real elocution. You must observe two directions which I shall give you: First, let your voices well out; next, you must observe and copy me and my gestures. Can you remember these?

No. 1.—Yes, sir; I think we can remember them; but how much shall we let our voices out. I am always afraid I shall bust something if I let my voice out too much.

P.—Well, sir, let me hear you speak, and then I can judge. Do you know, "On Linden when the sun was low"?

No. 1.—Yes; I know that.

P.—Well, you may speak it.

No. 1 (puts himself in a position, and in a very loud and high voice recites:)

"On Linden, when the sun was low,
All bloodless lay the untrodden snow,
And dark as winter was the flow
Of Iser rolling rapidly."

P. (*clapping his hands to his ears*).—Hold! enough, enough. Do you all speak as loud as that?

No. 4.—Just like that, sir.

P.—Well, then, I'll withdraw the rule requiring you to speak so loud as you can, and beg you instead to speak moderately—moderately, gentlemen. But you must be sure to move and act as you see me do. Our first selection will be from Shakespeare. I told you all to provide yourselves with mantles, since the ancient Romans, whom we are to personate, wore them. Under the present circumstances, I stated that your sisters' waterproof cloaks would answer every purpose.

No. 2.—I haven't any sister, Professor, so I got his sister (*pointing*) to lend me her waterproof. Will that do just as well?

P.—Certainly. Now throw them over your left arms.

(*In drawing them No. 3 accidentally hits No. 4, who, rubbing his arm, says:*)

No. 4.—What are you about, hitting around in that way? You've got to be more careful.

(*No. 1 also accidentally steps on the toes of No. 2, who limps around and makes great ado.*)

No. 2.—Oh! oh! my corns. What did you step on my corns for?

P.—Gentlemen, you must be more careful.

Nos. 2 and 4.—Why, we were just as careful as we could be. It's those fellows who aint careful.

P.—Now, then, gentlemen, in line, if you please, and follow my directions. But first, I'll recite, as appropriate to the occasion, Shakespeare's "Advice to the Players:"

"Speak the speech, I pray you, as I pronounce it to you; tripping on the tongue; but if you mouth it, as many of our players do, I had as lief the town crier spake my lines. Nor do not saw the air too much with your hand, thus, but use all gently." I repeat, gentlemen, be sure to imitate me: it is thus you will learn. Attention all: "If you have tears" (*throwing out right hand toward them*).

Class.—" If you have tears"—(*also throwing out their right hands with great animation*).

P.—" Prepare to shed them now," (*puts hands to eyes and whines and cries*).

C.—"Prepare to shed them now" (*also put hands, etc. In doing this,* No. 1 *hits* No. 2 *with his sword, and he calls out:*

No. 2.—Oh! why are you always hitting me? I'm half inclined to think you did it on purpose. I aint going to stand it any longer, unless I have the chance to do some hitting back.

P.—Silence, gentlemen. You must be willing to suffer something in the cause of education. "You all do know this mantle"—(*throwing out left arm and pointing with the right*).

C.—"You all do know this mantle"—(*same gestures; the various members dodging about as the swords are drawn*).

P.—"I remember the first time ever Cæsar put it on."

C.—"I remember the first time ever Cæsar put it on."

P.—"Look"—(*throwing out right hand*).

C.—"Look"—(*repeat gesture*).

P.—"In this place"—(*pointing*).

C.—"In this place"—(*pointing*).

P.—"Ran Cassius' dagger through."

C.—"Ran Cassius' dagger through."

P.—"See what a rent the envious Casca made—here" —(*pointing*).

C.—" See what a rent the envious Casca made—here"
—(*pointing*).

P.—" Thro' this the well-beloved Brutus stabbed"—
(*pointing*).

C.—" Thro' this the well-beloved Brutus stabbed"—
(*pointing*).

P.—" And as he plucked his cursed steel away"—
(*drawing sword back*).

C.—"And as he plucked his cursed steel away"—(*drawing swords back, and in so doing No. 1 hits No. 2, which causes him to double up and cry out in a whining way*).

No. 2.—There you go again, always hitting some one, you are. And I'm not going to stand your nonsense any longer.

P.—Silence there.

C.—Silence there. (*No. 2 calls out with the rest, though pretending to be in pain.*)

P. (*raising sword*).—Silence, I say!

C. (*raising sword*).—Silence, I say!

P.—Stop! stop! That is not found in the divine bard. Make ready, all. All ready?

C.—Ready.

P.—" Then burst his mighty heart"—(*left hand on heart, right arm over the eyes, pretending to weep*).

C.—" Then burst his mighty heart"—(*imitating gestures*).

P.—" And in his mantle muffling up his face"—(*folds cloak around his head*).

C.—"And in his mantle muffling up his face"—(*fold cloaks, etc.*)

P.—" Great Cæsar "—(*in a loud voice*).

C.—" Great Cæsar"—(*very loud*).

P.—" Fell "—(*going suddenly on his knees*).

C.—" Fell "—(*going down suddenly on their knees, and remain in this position about a minute*).

P. (*rising*).—Now, gentlemen, you have had your first lesson in real elocution, where everything is done that is spoken about in the piece itself. This one was intended to show you how an audience can be made to weep. The next will be to show you how it can be made to laugh. (*All bow.*)

KNOWING THE CIRCUMSTANCES.

CHARACTERS.—Five girls, from ten to twelve years of age: MAUD, an orphan, and very poorly clad; KATIE, ROSELLA, EDITH, and BELLE, daughters of wealthy parents.

SCENE.—*The five girls standing near each other,* MAUD *a little apart from the rest.*

Rosella.—O girls, my father has bought a beautiful sail-boat, and we expect to have a sail to-night upon the lake. Father gave me leave to invite a few of my friends to enjoy the sail with us. Will you go?

Katie, Edith, and Belle, together.—Oh! yes, yes, yes! Won't it be grand?

Katie.—Rosella, you are the best girl that ever was. [*Throws an arm around her.*]

Rosella.—Will you not go with us, Maud?

Maud (*glancing at her shabby dress and worn-out shoes*). —I would like to go, but fear I cannot. [*Turns to leave.*]

Rosella.—Come if you can, Maud.   [*Exit* MAUD.

Edith.—I cannot imagine why you are so anxious to have that ragged Maud Lindsey to be one of your sailing party.

Belle.—Nor I.

Katie.—Nor I.

Edith.—I don't believe she has anything fit to wear. Did you not see her glance at her dress when she replied to your question?

Rosella.—No; I did not notice it.

Katie.—How strange! I noticed it; didn't you, Belle?

Belle.—Yes, and I could not help pitying her, for I know she wanted to go so much.

Edith.—I can't believe it our duty to invite such a ragged thing everywhere. I think it bad enough to be obliged to associate with her at school.

Rosella.—O Edith! you surely cannot blame Maud for having no better clothing!

Edith.—I had no thought of blaming her; I only said I did not care to associate with her.

Katie.—I wonder if she has no better clothes.

Belle.—She had a better dress last summer.

Katie.—But we are talking about this summer.

[MAUD *appears on the stage and seems to be searching for something, but, not finding it, soon leaves.*]

Edith.—I wonder what she was looking after.

Belle.—She looked as if she had cried her eyes most out.

Katie.—That's nothing new; her eyes always look so.

Rosella.—I think we should all weep as much as Maud, if in her place. Mrs. Mason knows all about Maud and her parents, and says, if she was able, she would take her and do by her as by a child of her own.

Edith.—Did Mrs. Mason ever tell you about her?

Rosella.—Yes, she told me the other day.

Belle.—Tell us about her, Rosella.

Katie.—Yes, do.

Rosella.—I will, with pleasure. Maud's parents were very wealthy. They had two children besides Maud, a boy and a girl. One day her father came in looking very grave; he had failed. A few mornings after this, he awoke very ill. A physician was called, and his disease pronounced diphtheria. In a short time they were all ill with the same disease, and only Maud recovered.

[*A silence of some minutes.*]

Katie.—I have a dress at home which I think would fit Maud, and it is quite pretty.

Edith.—I have some boots. They don't come up quite as high around the ankle as I like to have them; but they are most new, and will look much better than her old ones.

Belle.—I will ask my mother to buy her a new hat; and I know she will, and some other things also.

Rosella.—I will also give her some articles of clothing, but what she needs most is our love. Shall we not give it to her.

All.—Yes, yes, she shall have our love.

[*Curtain falls.*

A SONG OF THE STATES.

Tune—My Native Land.
FOR FOURTEEN LITTLE GIRLS.

Each girl should be appareled in white, and one—the largest—so costumed as to represent the Goddess of Liberty. Each of the others should wear upon the head a band of pasteboard, bearing in gilt or silver letters the name of the State she represents, and carrying in the hand a small shield, which can also be made of pasteboard. Alternate stripes of white and red can be pasted lengthwise upon the shield within one-third of the distance from the top. On the one-third space, which must, of course, be blue, should be placed thirteen small white stars. On the reverse side may be fastened a strip of tape to enable the child to hold the shield during the performance.

ARRANGEMENT OF TABLEAU.—The Goddess may be placed on one side of the group, and arranged in such way as to look with pride on the original thirteen, and the smallest child, which should represent Rhode Island, might be kneeling at her feet, and holding in her hand a flag.

The performance can either be rendered as solo or as chorus, as may be best suited to the occasion.

DID you ever hear of Columbus,
   Who came out to the West—
Of all the mariners on earth
   The bravest and the best?

He mann'd his boats, and picked his crew,
   With spirits bold and brave,
Who, like himself, knew naught of fear,
   And crossed the ocean wave.

We thirteen sisters were the first
   To form into a band,
And represent the thirteen States
   First chartered in this land.

God bless the dauntless few who crossed
   The broad and rolling sea,
To give to us a happy home
   So wide, and rich, and free.

SPECIALTIES.

IN addition to our own publications herein mentioned, we make a specialty of supplying works relating to Elocution and Oratory, either in quantity or single copies. Orders for books upon any subject will receive our prompt attention and be filled upon most favorable terms.

For some time past we have felt the necessity of effecting an arrangement whereby we could supply the constant and increasing demand for

Special Selections.

It gives us great pleasure to announce that we now have facilities for filling this long-felt want. Selections are frequently read in public which please the audience and lead them to desire a copy, but not being personally acquainted with the reader, and knowing neither the author nor the publisher, they are at a loss to know how to proceed to obtain it. In most cases if the title be given us, or a short description of the selection, we can send the name and cost of the book in which the selection is found; and upon receipt of price, we will forward a copy of the work.

In a majority of cases however the selection is found in some of the paper-bound books of selections which sell at 30 cents. It will, therefore, save time and trouble to send the money with the inquiry.

The National School of Elocution and Oratory,

1124 ARCH STREET,

PUBLICATION DEPARTMENT,
CHAS. O. SHOEMAKER, MANAGER.

PHILADELPHIA.

ORATORY.

By REV. HENRY WARD BEECHER.

Neatly Bound, Cloth, 40 Cents.

THE attention of all persons interested in the Art of Expression is invited to our new issue of Henry Ward Beecher's unique and masterly exposition of the fundamental principles of true oratory.

"Training in this department," said Beecher, "is the great want of our day; for we are living in a land whose genius, whose history, whose institutions, whose people, eminently demand oratory."

It must be conceded that few men ever enjoyed a wider experience or achieved a higher reputation in the realm of public oratory than Mr. Beecher. What he had to say on this subject was born of experience, and his own inimitable style was at once both statement and illustrative of his theme.

From *The School Journal*, New York City:—"Richly freighted with the golden fruit of observation, experience, sympathy, understanding, knowledge, and reason."

Sold by all Booksellers, or mailed upon receipt of price.

The National School of Elocution and Oratory,

1124 ARCH STREET,

PUBLICATION DEPARTMENT,
CHAS. O. SHOEMAKER, MANAGER.

PHILADELPHIA.

CHOICE ⊙ HUMOR.

For Reading and Recitation.

ADAPTED FOR USE IN PUBLIC AND PRIVATE.

The Latest and best Book of Humor Published.

200 Pages.   Appropriately Engraved Cover.

Paper Binding, 30 Cents; Boards, 50 Cents.

AS its name implies, the selections are chosen with the greatest care, avoiding the coarse and vulgar on the one hand, and the flat and insipid on the other.

The Publishers possess unequaled facilities for securing the best readings of every character, and the present volume may be considered without a rival.

The pieces are new, but few of them having previously appeared in any similar publication, and the range of subjects is unusually wide.

The repertoires of many of the best amateur and professional readers have been examined, and the choicest bits of humor have been carefully culled and bound up in this rich, golden sheaf, and are here offered to the public for the first time in book form.

The book contains eighty-five pieces, is clearly printed on good, strong paper, and is bound in a handsome and appropriately engraved cover. Sold everywhere, or mailed upon receipt of price.

The National School of Elocution and Oratory,

1124 ARCH STREET,

PUBLICATION DEPARTMENT,
CHAS. O. SHOEMAKER, MANAGER.

PHILADELPHIA.

Child's Own Speaker.

FOR CHILDREN OF FIVE YEARS.

100 Pieces, Attractively Bound.

Paper Binding, 15 cts.;   Boards, 25 cts.

THIS little book is a collection of Recitations, Motion Songs, Concert Pieces, Dialogues, and Tableaux, for the very little children of five years old and thereabouts. In all, it contains 100 pieces, many of which are entirely new as well as novel in arrangement, and have been specially written for this book.

While keeping in mind the tender age of the little ones for whom this collection is intended, we have excluded from it mere baby-talk, and have inserted only such pieces as contain some thought worth memorizing.

The contents will be found to be varied, fresh, childlike, and entertaining, and of such a nature as to be adapted to almost every occasion.

"Its selections are admirably adapted to amuse and instruct those for whose use it is intended."—*Interior, Chicago.*

Sold by all Booksellers and Newsdealers, or mailed upon receipt of price.

The National School of Elocution and Oratory,

1124 ARCH STREET,

Publication Department,
Chas. C. Shoemaker, Manager.   PHILADELPHIA.

Best Things from Best Authors,

Volumes 1, 2, 3, 4, and 5 issued.

Designed for use in Schools and Colleges and for Public and Social Entertainment.

---

600 PAGES, CLOTH BOUND, EACH, $1.50.

☞ SPECIAL.—For a limited time we are offering the full set of five volumes, put up in neat and durable boxes, at the *special price* of $5.00; the regular price would be $7.50.

EACH volume is composed of three numbers of *The Elocutionist's Annual* in the order of their issue, thus comprising the latest and best productions of the most popular English and American writers of to-day, together with the **choicest selections of standard literature** adapted to reading in public and private; and is so arranged with indexes and classifications of selections, authors, etc., as to make it not only one of the most valuable collections of choice readings ever published, but one of the most **complete as a book of ready reference.**

H. J. Greenwell, A M, Principal Bardstown Male and Female Institute, Bardstown, Ky., says: "A work eminently suited to school-room purposes as well as for all departments of elocutionary drill."

White Sunlight of Potent Words.

An oration by Rev. John S. MacIntosh, D. D. Delivered before the National School of Elocution and Oratory, June 15th, 1881. Cloth, 25 cents.

The above books for sale by all Booksellers, or will be sent upon receipt of price by the Publishers,

The National School of Elocution and Oratory,

1124 ARCH STREET,

PUBLICATION DEPARTMENT,
CHAS. C. SHOEMAKER, MANAGER.

PHILADELPHIA.

Choice * Dialogues

FOR

School and Social Entertainment.

*12mo. Handsomely Engraved Cover. Paper Binding,
30 Cents. Boards, 50 Cents.*

THIS volume has been prepared in response to many urgent and repeated requests. The topics have been arranged on a comprehensive plan, with reference to securing the greatest possible variety, and the matter has been prepared especially for us by a corps of able writers. Each production has been critically examined as to its moral tone, its literary structure and expression, and its adaptation to the purpose intended.

In the preparation of these Dialogues, provision has been made for all seasons and occasions—Private Entertainments, Sunday and Day School Exhibitions, Holidays, Anniversaries, National and Patriotic Celebrations, Temperance Meetings, etc., etc.

"We have read much of this book, and know of nothing else so well suited to school and social purposes."—*Christian Statesman,* Milwaukee, Wis.

Sold by all Booksellers and Newsdealers or mailed upon receipt of price.

The National School of Elocution and Oratory,

1124 ARCH STREET,

PUBLICATION DEPARTMENT
CHAS. O. SHOEMAKER, MANAGER

PHILADELPHIA

Elocutionary Charts.

OUTLINE OF ELOCUTION.

A large wall chart, 60x72 inches, handsomely mounted.

THE arrangement of this chart is striking and suggestive, and presents a clear and practical analysis of the whole subject. Beginning with the definition of elocution, it proceeds to treat of its importance, of conversation as its basis, of principles, and of methods of instruction. The outline of these topics, with their natural subdivisions, will enable the teacher to proceed systematically with the work of instruction, and will, at the same time, assist the student to an intelligent comprehension of the subject.

TABLE OF VOCAL EXERCISES.

A small wall chart, 32x44 inches, handsomely mounted.

The distinctive aims of this chart are to secure purity, power, flexibility, and character of tone. Beginning with the long vowel sounds, natural or conversational, it proceeds to the systematic cultivation of the voice, in response to the whole field of sentiment and passion. Then by a carefully arranged set of sentences these principles are immediately applied to expression, thus securing to the student such facility in their use as will enable him to apply them in conversation, in reading, or in public address.

PRICES: { *Outline of Elocution,* $5.00
Table of Vocal Exercises. . . $2.00

Sold by all Booksellers, or sent, prepaid, upon receipt of price.

The National School of Elocution and Oratory,

Publication Department,
Chas. C. Shoemaker, Manager.

1124 ARCH STREET,

PHILADELPHIA.

Little People's Speaker.

FOR CHILDREN OF TEN YEARS.

100 PAGES, HANDSOMELY ENGRAVED COVER.

Paper Binding, 15 cts.;   Boards, 25 cts.

ADAPTED to children of **ten years of age**, and suited to every occasion in which the little folks are called upon to take part.

Bright and witty child-thoughts, often tersely and beautifully expressed, and ranging in length from four to twenty lines, will please the wee ones. Motion Songs, Concert Recitations, Holiday Pieces, Ringing Temperance Speeches, and Soul-stirring Patriotic Orations will delight the older boys and girls.

A number of these pieces have been written specially for this book, and all are fresh and new.

"This book is adapted to all kinds of juvenile entertainments, and will supply a widely increasing demand for selections for the little ones."—*Herald, Syracuse, N. Y.*

Sold by all Booksellers and Newsdealers, or mailed upon receipt of price.

The National School of Elocution and Oratory,

1124 ARCH STREET,

PUBLICATION DEPARTMENT.
CHAS. C. SHOEMAKER, MANAGER.

PHILADELPHIA.

www.ingramcontent.com/pod-product-compliance
Lightning Source LLC
Chambersburg PA
CBHW020143170426
43199CB00010B/866